Taking You From Surviving To Thriving

The Essential Moving Guide For Families

Practical Advice To Ease Your Transition

And Create A Sense Of Belonging

By **Sara Elizabeth Boehm**

Cover Design: Ashley Boehm
Photo: Getty Images, Steve Cole Images

First Edition

Available for bulk purchases in the U.S. by corporations,
institutions, and other organizations. For more information, please
contact our Customer Support Department
at support@myessentialguide.com

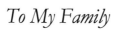

To My Family

Contents

Introduction

Creating a Smooth Transition and Sense of Belonging

We're moving! Those two words can cause everything else in life to come to a standstill and incite fear, anxiety, and a myriad of other emotions. Moving can be fun—change brings anticipation, excitement, and opportunity. On the flip side, moving is also tiring, depressing, and often lonely and uncomfortable. Those who leave and those who stay behind are both affected by those two words.

Children and adults are both affected by a move; however, it may be more challenging for children, as they haven't developed coping mechanisms to deal with new situations. Whether it's a young child who needs structure and consistency or a pre-teen or teen whose social circles are of great importance, moving, like many types of change, upsets life's balance.

Between the ages of two and 14, I heard those words six times. Moving six times growing up and then another six times post-college, I had the chance to see almost every region of the country throughout my formative years. I wasn't a gregarious or outgoing child, so be assured an outgoing nature isn't necessary to successfully move and acclimate. I survived the worst aspects of moving and prospered with some of the advantages it can generate. As an adult, I can now see how moving during my childhood affected me and shaped the person I've become. So why write this book? I once heard a story on an episode of *West

Wing that has stuck with me ever since: *A guy is walking down the street and falls in a hole. The walls are so steep he can't get out. A doctor passes by and the guy shouts up, "Hey you. Can you help me out?" The doctor writes a prescription, throws it down in the hole and moves on. Then a priest comes along and the guy shouts up, "Father, I'm down in this hole can you help me out?" The priest writes out a prayer, throws it down in the hole and moves on. Then a friend walks by, "Hey Joe, it's me, can you help me out?" And the friend jumps in the hole. The guy says, "Are you stupid? Now we're both down here." The friend says, "Yeah, but I've been down here before and I know the way out."* That's why we are all here—to share our experiences and help one another along.

This book seeks to offer some practical advice and insights based upon my own experiences. My family and friends, including those who've moved frequently and those who've moved once, those who've moved domestically and those who've moved internationally, have added their insights and thoughts as well. While moving impacts the lives of everyone involved, if you have children, you worry about the long and short-term effects it will have on their lives. Your children will look to you for support in coping with the stress of the relocation. I've written this book to encourage you, provide guidance on how to survive the move, and show you practical ways to support and guide your family through a smooth transition before, during, and after the move. As I reflected on my own moves and reached out to others about their experiences, I began to research the impact moving has on children. Surprisingly, there's little information available on this subject, considering it affects so many (for a research summary, see Appendix I). What is clear though is that when efforts are made to help and support a child throughout relocation, the child greatly benefits. The fact that you are reading this book already suggests you are preparing to meet the challenges relocation will bring to you and your family.

The Benefits of Moving: What Moving Has Taught Me

Although there are many difficulties associated with a move, there are also ways that, in the long-term, your child (and even you) can benefit from the relocation. Before tackling the challenges, which easily come to mind, let's discuss how a move can positively impact you and your children as they grow into adulthood. In my experience, although moving was distressing at times, there were clearly some advantages which I did benefit from. Below is a list I, and many others whom I've talked to over the years, believe are the benefits of moving (particularly moving as a child).

Instills confidence

First and foremost, a successful move will bring about a feeling of accomplishment, which facilitates confidence. You can gain confidence in yourself and what you can achieve, independence in knowing you have made it through a difficult time, and assurance that you can handle new situations. In the stories people have shared with me, this is often the first thing that comes to mind as a "takeaway" for those who have moved and for those observing people in their lives who have relocated. People who relocate are often more confident in themselves and more independent. Lisa, a friend of mine, moved when she was 10 years old. She returned home from her first day at her new school and triumphantly informed her mother, "That was scary, but I made it through. I can do anything now."

Increases your ability to handle uncertainty and new situations

Often, after experiencing the changes that accompany a move and identifying what worked to get them through it, those who relocate tend to be less fearful of new situations and more willing to take on new experiences which require a lot of change. When you're forced to confront change and try things on your own, you learn how to be more adaptable and flexible, how to live in different environments, and how to operate within different systems. You also learn to be less fearful of change because you've discovered coping mechanisms to deal with it. Learning to handle change can open up doors for you and your children in the future. There's power in knowing you don't have to be shackled to your current situation and can embrace new opportunities as they come to you. Melissa, a former colleague of mine, would often talk about watching her son Tyler interact with other children in new situations. Their family moved twice in four years. After the first move Melissa took Tyler to soccer tryouts and watched as he nervously stayed on the sidelines and waited for others to interact with him. After experiencing the transition Melissa would joke that he was like a different child during that second move. She dropped him off for soccer tryouts in their new city and, while he was still a bit nervous, he knew more of what to expect so he ran on to the field and began engaging with the other children. Melissa attributed some of this to maturing but also some to the experiences he had during the first move, better equipping him to handle the uncertainty of the second move.

As your children enter adulthood, their ability to adapt to change will make it easier for them to leave for college, start a new job, travel, and join groups and teams because they've experienced being the "new kid," adjusting, and making friends. Few people like change, but those who've experienced it know they can get through it and aren't afraid to move or to introduce change into their lives as they get older. And you don't have to be a child to benefit; even adults routinely state this as an advantage of their own moving experiences.

Helps you gain self-awareness

Moving to a new city, state, or country provides you with the opportunity to try new things and learn about yourself. As I moved around during my childhood, I quickly learned that rather than jumping into new situations, I prefer to take some time to observe and get a feel for the environment. Others can misconstrue this as standoffish. So, while I can't change my preference, I learned to balance it by smiling while I observed, to seem more approachable. I also discovered the effectiveness of opening up and being honest and vulnerable about my newness, to reassure others I wasn't judging them but was merely adjusting to my new surroundings.

Self-awareness is essential for success (no matter how you define success), and moving yields great opportunities to get to know yourself. You find out how you react when your safety net is gone. You learn to understand what you miss, what you value, and what you look for when building new friendships and relationships. I learned more about who I was and what mattered to me from my childhood moves than from most of the other major events in my life. Moving forces you to try new things and in the process you learn what you like and what you don't like.

You're also able to learn, firsthand, the importance of choosing a positive mindset and attitude. You'll learn you're in control of your situation and you have the ability to take charge and make it better. That knowledge and self-empowerment not only teaches you about yourself but will serve you well as you make future decisions and face new situations.

Broadens your perspective

Moving allows you to see and experience so much more than you would have if you had remained in one location. The experience comes down to what you make of it. You may not like a city, but it, like anywhere else, has its advantages and disadvantages. If your new location was really that awful, no one would live there. People often ask me, "What place was your favorite?" Even when my family asks those questions of one another (e.g., "name your favorite house"), we always have to break it down into components. There was no "best house", but there was the house with the best yard, the house with the best living room, kitchen, basement, etc. The same goes for our favorite city or school. No specific one wins overall, they all had great things we loved and missed when we left and things we'd like to have changed. Moving gives you the perspective to see and experience the differences between places and to appreciate them.

In addition to experiencing new places and things, you meet new people who you'll connect with, enjoy, and value. The true friendships you forge will stand the test of time and distance. You may fall out of contact with some friends, but your life will have been greatly enriched by meeting and getting to know them. I'm blessed to have friends across the country. I've learned every region has great people—people who are worth opening up to and letting into your life. It may not always feel like it but, I assure you, they're out there. Ultimately, it's the people in your life who matter. If you develop a strong support network, it doesn't really matter where you are.

You can make friends anywhere. You can be happy anywhere. We all benefit from new experiences throughout our lives, no matter our age. They help us develop a broader perspective on life, ourselves, and others. My mother distinctly remembers talking to a friend of hers before we moved from Philadelphia to Syracuse. This friend was the wife of a local doctor and upon hearing we were moving surprised my mother by saying how lucky my mother was to get to move and experience a new place. She said that while she loved the area and loved her husband's practice, it was a private practice that would be hard to re-build in a new location so she would never have the opportunity to leave that suburb of Philadelphia and try out a new area. My mother left that lunch with a renewed perspective on our upcoming move.

Strengthens family bonds

In many ways, a move forces family members to rely upon each other and, as a result, the family gets closer. In particular, families depend more on each other in the early days of the move while outside friendships are being established. During this time, you create collective memories for the long-term and develop your family story. In our family photo albums we would document each house and our memories there. We often talk about the places we've lived and what we liked the best. To this day, during each winter holiday season, we make a point of talking through our family story. It's a bond we share; no one else has the unique memories we have experienced. It's one of the threads that tie us together. I don't think I would be as close with my family today if we hadn't gone through those experiences together. Just like all memories in life, some parts are happy, some parts are sad, and some parts are funny, but our shared experience is our bond.

Provides an opportunity for a fresh start

Moving is a fresh start, a time to try out things you've always wanted to do (or that you may not have even known about). With each new experience, new doors are opened and new opportunities are presented to us. Let your children know they can use this opportunity to try new things: new sports, clubs, or activities and break away from any stereotype they may have had in the last place. I took advantage of the moves to try out different areas: from dance to orchestra, from running track to debate team, from not participating in class to trying to speak up more. For one move, I cut my long hair short to try out a new look with a group of people who would have never known me any other way. Each move gave me the chance to learn what I like to do, but it also gave me the chance to learn about what I truly value in myself and in others. When I found myself in one of the junior high cliques that was more exclusive and unkind to others, I quickly course-corrected and was sure to be more careful in who I chose to surround myself with during the next move. I tried to use each move as an opportunity to try something I had always wanted to do and see if I enjoyed it. It's also an opportunity, like New Year's, to make a resolution to fix the things that need to be fixed. If your child fell in with the wrong crowd in the old school, this could be a chance to start again. If your child was struggling in a class and felt others' expectations for him or her were low, you can find a tutor to help your child break out of the old mold. Changing one's behavior takes work and support, so it won't be easy, but starting with a clean slate is like a "get out of jail free" card. No reputation, baggage, or expectations, just a fresh start and a new chapter to be written.

From fun, small changes to larger personal goals, use the move as a starting point. This is a chance to change what you do, not change the fundamentals of who you are. Many people just let life happen to them rather than taking the reins and driving it in the direction they want to go. Life will throw all kinds of things at you, but you always have the power to take action and change directions if you don't like where you're headed. It's important to know what matters to you and where you want to be in life. If you don't know this now, take some time to think about what you want and how to get it. From spending more time with your family, to career goals, to picking up a new hobby or language, if you want to make it happen, you need to clearly identify it as a goal and start setting smaller goals that will get you closer to your ultimate goal. Make your goals measurable and set a time frame for achieving them. Then communicate them to those who you trust and who will encourage you and hold you accountable.

Have your children think through any changes they would like to make. If complicated, encourage them to create a plan for how they're going to go about doing so. Remind them that things will take time and to be realistic in their expectations. Encourage them to believe that they can rise to the challenge, will learn about themselves in the process, and will learn to embrace new opportunities. Teaching your children to try new things and not to fear failure can be two of the best gifts you give them to equip them for success later in life. Your children will start to see that even when things are seemingly out of their control, they can still control their actions to make the best of the situation they are in.

Teaches you how to make friends and intentionally connect with others

Another practical skill you'll develop is how to make friends, an essential skill that is sometimes challenging. Practice makes perfect, and moving provides you a great chance to practice connecting with others and building a support network for yourself. With each attempt, you'll get better at reaching out to others, determining what you value in friendships, learning how to meaningfully connect with others, and building upon those connections. We all need other people, and the sooner we can learn how to intentionally surround ourselves with healthy, supportive people in any situation, the better off we'll be for the rest of our lives.

I can still remember when I was in seventh grade and my extended family was visiting for the holidays. I had just moved, yet again, and my cousin asked me how it was going. I politely responded that it was hard but that each week was getting a bit better. She looked at me earnestly and said, "I just think sometimes about how lucky you are. I've lived in the same place my entire life and would have no idea how to go somewhere new and make friends and build a whole new life for myself. You know how to do that." Up until that point I'd never given much thought to the benefits of moving. Moving was a fact of life and I had plodded through it, but my cousin's comment took me by surprise. While her comment may partially have been due to a "grass is always greener" syndrome, over time it really resonated with me that I was picking up life skills I could not only use later in life but from which I was already benefiting.

~~~~~~~~~~~~~~~~

Life will throw a lot at you. During a move, it often feels like life throws more at you than you can handle. Moving is a turning point in our lives. It's an event which doesn't seem completely real until you come face-to-face with it. Life is handing you an opportunity, but with it comes challenges. In the following sections you'll find practical advice on what you can expect before, during, and after your move. You'll find suggestions and simple strategies, as well as coping mechanisms to help you and your children complete this move successfully. Every move is unique because every family is unique. Read the parts you find helpful, and skip the sections which aren't as useful to your situation and family and although you'll get a few curve balls, you'll find the transition will be easier than you expected.

Part I: Before the Move

Chapter 1: Telling Your Children

"Sometimes the questions are complicated and the answers are simple." — Dr. Seuss

If you've decided to move, the next big step is telling your children. You may be nervous about what to say and how they'll react, so here are some suggestions to help communicate the news openly and honestly.

Tell your children before telling others

Your children need to hear the news from you—their parents who love and care about them and who can best explain how the move will affect them. Don't tell your friends, family, and neighbors until after you tell your children. Even a casual conversation about a possible interview could get back to your children and alarm them. Most of us can think of times in our lives when we've heard news from another source before hearing it from those close to us and how we felt betrayed, scared, or confused.

It's important to recognize your children will start to sense something is happening, so tell them as soon as you can. You certainly don't want to break the news too soon and risk getting them worked up and worried over nothing if things aren't certain and may fall through. When you feel the move is likely to occur and need to start openly planning and communicating your plans to others, let your children know. You may think you can hide it, but children will pick up on even subtle signs: tension, whispering, and closed door conversations. There were a few moves I can remember in my own childhood where I approached my parents because it just felt to me like we might be moving again. Was I psychic? No. Did I even recognize what I was picking up on? Not usually. But I did notice something was happening without even realizing what had caused me to be suspicious.

Find the appropriate place and time

As for the how, where, or when, it's important to take into consideration how your children tend to react. If the younger ones look to the oldest child for guidance, consider telling your oldest first so he or she will be able to support your younger children when you tell them. If you know one of your children will require more attention, consider telling him or her separately so you can give them your undivided attention. Also, consider the setting and time of day. You'll likely want to tell them at home, where they'll feel most comfortable expressing their feelings. Tell them when you both have time to talk things through, not right before their school day begins or before bedtime. My parents would sometimes tell my sister and I together and sometimes tell us the news separately, but they would always give us the chance to react and respond. If the move is non-negotiable, sometimes it's best to just dive straight in (e.g., "I've got some news I want to talk through with you that will affect our family. We're going to be moving to Chicago in a few weeks").

Be honest and provide details

The more information you can give your children, the better. You don't want them to be in a state of limbo, drowning in a sea of unknowns. Help them cope by providing them with as much information as you can (why you're moving, where, when, what it means for them, how you'll get there, where you'll live). Don't assume that because they're children they won't worry about the details. They'll want to know everything, if only to be assured and reminded that things aren't out of control, you're thinking about them, and you're aware of how the move will impact their lives. Think of a time in your life when a corporate reorganization was announced as imminent but had not yet occurred, or when you were waiting to hear back from an organization about a job offer. Remember the situations where you've been in limbo because you didn't know all of the information others knew. It's very stressful and exhausting to play out all of the potential outcomes in your mind. It's far better to know the news, good or bad, so you can start adjusting and dealing with it. Your goal is to show your children they're an important part of the move and their concerns are your concerns. Saying things like, "We know how much you love your guitar lessons here, so we'll be sure to find you another good instructor after we move," will remind them you love and care about them and help to calm their anxieties.

Be honest but positive. You want to present the information in a way that highlights what's happening in a factual and supportive manner. On the flip side, you don't want to paint an overly optimistic picture. A positive, upbeat attitude is different than making promises you can't fulfill. Use the opportunity to connect and share your feelings with your children. They'll value your authenticity and see that you can still be positive even while you share their feelings of apprehension about the move. This is also the time to tell your children how you came to the decision to move and what matters most to your family (we value staying together, we value supporting one another, we value new experiences, we value staying in touch with our loved ones, etc.). If you think you'll forget something, make a list and refer to it during the conversation.

> **Helpful information to provide:**
> -*Where you are moving* (show on a map, mention points of interest or what is nearby)
> -*When each part of the move will occur* (move out, move in, any temporary housing dates, and how this will affect their schooling, activities, etc.)
> -*Why you are moving* (provide a bit of background to give context to the move and to allow your children to understand your decision process)
> -*How the pieces of the move will occur* (who will do the packing and moving, how you will travel to your new home, how and when you will be house hunting, etc.)

As you are thinking about what to say and what information to share, tailor your message to your children:

Younger Children: Younger children's lives primarily revolve around the family home and they tend to be less dependent upon their friends. While you'll need to assure them they'll make new friends, you'll also want to focus on family, school, and consistency as you reassure them. Remind them that the family will stay together and that you'll be there to support them. Talk about your new home and what it will or may have (a playroom, a swing set, etc.) or your new town and any fun sites that will be nearby. Talk about their new school and how they'll have a good teacher they'll like or activities and clubs they'll be eager to join.

Pre-teens/Teens: As children grow older, their friends begin to take a central role in their life and their identity, and this is when moving can become more emotional and difficult from a social standpoint. Emphasize how important the move is to the family so they can see the bigger picture and involve them as much as possible so they're able to have some control over the situation. Go into the discussion with an understanding of how this will impact your teen's life. Ask questions, provide relevant information, and involve them, or be open to involving them, in areas that are important to them. Even if you have a teenager acting out against the move and you're frustrated with their behavior, don't let the frustration win. Patiently be there for them as they react, and once they've stated their objections, continue to support them and seek to understand their concerns and feelings without arguing with them. For more on teenagers, see Chapter 4.

Keep up an on-going dialogue and provide regular updates

Although the final decision may not change, don't let your children get the feeling the subject isn't open for further discussion or questions. They'll process the information in their own time and may have additional questions or need support along the way. You won't have all of the answers nor will you have perfect responses. What matters most is that your children feel included and know they can come to you at any time, as things come up.

Likewise, as things come up on your end and you get more information about the move, continue to share with them and give them status updates. Remember, there are logistical elements of the move (When are the movers coming?) and there are emotional aspects (How will I make new friends?). You'll need to address both of these areas with your children on a regular basis.

- Tell your children before telling others.

- Find the appropriate place and time.

- Be honest and provide details.

- Keep an on-going dialogue and provide regular updates.

Chapter 2: Listening and Supporting

"The single biggest problem with communication is the illusion that it has taken place." — George Bernard Shaw

Communication is critical in all aspects of our lives and essential throughout the relocation process, both before and after the move. Listening is one of the key elements to effectively communicating. Check in with your children, ask them how they're doing, and pay attention to verbal and non-verbal cues. Don't assume how they're feeling; genuinely observe and listen to your children with the goal of understanding them.

Listen first and don't judge

Each child is different and will struggle in different areas; how he or she responds is entirely individualistic and dependent upon the situation. There's no way to predict how children will react or a specific timeline for when they'll work through their issues. Some children may struggle early on and some may not have any issues until weeks after the move. Some children may have a very emotional reaction and others may keep things bottled up inside. Moving brings up a host of emotions, many of them conflicting, for both children and adults. Sadness over leaving loved ones, familiar faces and places, fear and anxiety of the unknown, anger at having your world turned upside down, and feeling that you'll be all alone from this point on are all normal reactions. There's also the excitement of starting fresh and experiencing new things. This may be one of the first times your children have dealt with this type of situation so it's important to encourage them to share their feelings. Your role is to listen and not judge them when they do share with you. Show them change is exciting but also that sadness is a normal part of grieving a loss. Let them know it's okay to have conflicting feelings about the move. Give them permission to feel how they feel, even if you don't understand it. Remember, as an adult, you have some control over the situation and your life, but they're in a position where they don't have any control and that's a rough place to be.

As you listen to your children express their feelings toward the move, don't try to change their minds. You're trying to understand and acknowledge their feelings. If your child is crying, sit with him, hug him, and let him know things may be hard for a little while but they will get better in time. If your child is angry, be patient with her, acknowledge that her life is going to be affected, and listen for the concerns hiding beneath her anger and frustration. Children need to feel heard and understood—jumping to tell them what they "should" do or feel will make them feel dismissed and disregarded. You may be eager to reach the stage of reassuring and problem solving, but you can't effectively help your children until they feel understood. Then and only then can you both start working together to address their concerns and worries.

George Bernard Shaw said, "The single biggest problem with communication is the illusion that it has taken place." There is a powerful truth behind this message: it sums up many of the misunderstandings and conflicts we've had with family and friends, in relationships at work, and at school. Communicating can't just be about talking; it has more than one key element. Honest and straightforward sharing is one component, but truly listening with the intent to understand (not thinking of your next response) is the most critical part of communicating. Don't make assumptions; listen to understand, and ask follow up questions to make sure you really get it.

Once your children have reacted and feel understood, they'll begin directing their energy toward asking questions. Your role is to support them and love them and later, when they're ready, teach them the strategies they'll need to best tackle their new circumstances.

Mark, a family friend, remembers making a move in junior high. When his parents let him know about their upcoming move he was really upset. His parents assumed it was because he didn't want to leave his friends. "While I obviously didn't want to move away from my friends, I was most concerned with something else. I was on the football team and loved it even though I wasn't a particularly strong player. We were moving to a school in Texas where football was a big deal, and I doubted that I would be able to make the team. I was then being forced to give up that part of myself. I enjoyed playing; I enjoyed being on the team and placing some of my identity in that." When I asked if he told his parents he went on to explain, "It was silly, but it mattered so much at the time. And my parents just didn't get that. I didn't try very hard to explain it to them because I thought they would think it was stupid, but I wish I had. Once we got to Texas I saw there were a few smaller school districts where we could have looked and I would likely have been able to make the team and keep that part of my life."

Help your children identify and work through their worries and fears

As your children think about the upcoming changes, they may begin to develop fears about a variety of things. It's important to teach your children the power of sharing their fears. When fears stay bottled up inside our minds they can grow and take on a life of their own. When we begin to communicate those fears, we can take some control and figure out ways to address them and make them seem more manageable and less ominous. As a parent, you have the opportunity to be a role model for your children and teach them coping skills they'll be able to use throughout their lives.

Fears. Have your children talk out or write down their worries and fears about the move. You can then go through the list together and address each fear one by one. Some of their worries may not be able to be answered immediately (Are we taking our pet with us?), some you can research or help your children research on their own (Does my new school have a soccer team? When are tryouts?), and others you can handle by helping them think about strategies to implement. I would often worry each time that I wouldn't be able to make friends at my new school. My father would sit with me, listen to my concerns and then talk about other times I was new. He would remind me of the other schools I had attended, when I joined the local tennis team, and when I took dance lessons, gently repeating how I had made good friends in each instance even though I had worried. Then he would also remind me that it was easy to make friends by introducing yourself to others and being friendly and approachable. Talking things out helped bring a dose of reality to the fear I was feeling. It sounds simple, but even writing down or saying our fears out loud can lessen the power they have over us.

What they'll miss/What they're looking forward to.
Encourage your children to think about the things they'll miss most and then write them down. Along with keeping a journal or blog, suggest other outlets to express their feelings—music, dance, painting, writing a song, making a comic book. Whatever medium your children prefer, find a way they can use it to express and work through their feelings. Also, ask them to try focusing on the things they're excited about. Whether it's their new room, the mountains or the ocean that will be nearby, or the opportunity to meet new people, there's always something to look forward to. They can even consider what they won't miss or are happy to leave behind (neighbors or classmates they weren't crazy about or not sharing a bedroom anymore). Ask them to express their

feelings and share yours in return. Be open and honest with them about what you'll miss so they'll feel comfortable being open with you. Talk with them about past examples of times when you've felt similarly (when you were new to a group, job, or school, or when you moved somewhere new) and how you dealt with it. This provides them with coping mechanisms and the confidence that they can make it through this difficult period, just as you and others did in the past.

What makes them comfortable. Have your children make a list of the things that make them feel happy and safe. Be sure those items are with them throughout the move or can be quickly and easily unpacked upon arrival. My sister would always want her teddy bear with her. We made sure that Teddy was always set aside and not packed and that her other stuffed animals were in a box labeled accordingly so we could find them quickly at the new house. For the people and items you won't be able to take with you (grandma, friends), explain to your children why and create a plan of action on how they can stay in touch as well as develop similar attachments in the new place, like a new best friend.

Suggest they make a scrapbook of their current home and friends as a way to help them find closure and take their memories with them. They can include pictures of their favorite places and people and ask their friends to write notes or letters to take with them to remind them of the things they love. Also, consider making plans for a return visit so your children will have something to look forward to. Don't return too soon after the move; children need time to adjust to their new home and school so they will miss it during the return visit. For more on return visits, see Chapter 14.

What they're grateful for. It's often helpful to have your children think about the things they're grateful for. We often forget how lucky we are and may need to remind ourselves to appreciate what we do have in the midst of challenging times.

Suggestions for journal topics:
- Thinking about moving makes me feel. . . .
- The hardest part of the move will be. . . .
- The things I will miss most when I move. . .
- The things I will not miss when I move. . .
- Questions I have about the move or my new home or school...
- Once I have moved, I am excited about. . .
- I am nervous about. . .
- Three things I am grateful for are. . .
- Things that I want to take with me on our moving journey...
- Think about a time in the past when you were new to a situation. What did you do? What else could you have done?

Be observant

Don't assume just because your children haven't brought things to you they're not struggling. Ask questions and touch base periodically. If they don't want to open up to you, encourage them to reach out to their friends, teachers, coaches, or other family members such as grandparents, aunts, and uncles. I had a friend who really struggled with finding out she had to move. She didn't want to talk to her parents so she set up some time to talk to our guidance counselor at school and felt a bit better after discussing the move with him. Consider reaching out to those adults close to them to see how they think the news and adjustment is going.

It's important to remain observant throughout the process and watch for non-verbal cues that may indicate your child is suffering from depression. Don't be afraid to seek professional help if needed. On the flip side, don't overly worry and look for things which aren't there, but do pay attention to any unusual and unexpected changes in mood and/or behavior.

Depression can manifest itself in different ways, especially in children. Crying, moping, yelling, hitting, bedwetting, tantrums, or retreating from relationships are all indicators there's something wrong. Your children may say they're okay with the move but at the same time they may be losing sleep, their grades may be slipping, they may try to avoid talking about it, or they may experience a loss of appetite. If you're worried about how your child is handling the move, talk to him or her, and consider seeking the help of a school guidance counselor, doctor, or recommended therapist.

- **Listen first and don't judge.**
- **Help your children identify and work through their worries and fears.**
- **Be observant.**

Chapter 3: Choose to View it as an Adventure

"Happiness is not something ready made. It comes from your own actions."
— Dalai Lama XIV

"Change your thoughts and you change your world." *— Norman Vincent Peale*

One of the most important things you can do for yourself and your children during the move is to choose to view it as an adventure. In reality, you really are embarking on an adventure. The Merriam-Webster dictionary defines adventure as, "an exciting or remarkable experience". You're headed to a new place and have an opportunity to start fresh and experience entirely new things. Encourage your children to look forward to the surprises they'll encounter on their new adventure.

Do you remember the *Choose Your Own Adventure* books from years ago? This is the time to write your own—every choice you make on your journey will add another chapter, and at the end, you'll have pages of memories to share with your family for years to come.

A positive mindset is one of the most powerful tools at your disposal

Our thoughts are powerful; they shape our feelings, our outlook, our reactions, our actions and our decisions. Intentionally choosing to have a positive mindset will be a game changer for you and for your children. While this is much easier said than done, it's absolutely worth the effort. Choosing to be positive will affect how you act and how you unconsciously start to view your new world.

Research tells us our mindset will influence our actions and will ultimately affect our beliefs. If you tell yourself you can't do something over and over again, you'll never even attempt to try it. Study after study has proven the impact our thoughts have on our behavior. When you think positive thoughts, you're more likely to experience positive outcomes.

Having trouble mustering up positive thoughts? Research has also shown that taking positive actions can bring about positive thoughts. Behave as if you're enjoying things. Go out and meet people and try new things even if you aren't feeling excited about it. Smiling and acting excited, confident, or interested may produce those emotions.

If you make a conscious effort to think and act like the move is an adventure, you'll be prepared to meet any challenges along the way. I had a former manager who always used to tell his employees, "If a situation makes you feel nervous or awkward, smile and act like it doesn't, eventually you will forget that you were feeling that way." I remember one of my co-workers rolling his eyes at the advice, but a few months later he recounted a presentation he was asked to do. It was to a larger group than he was used to working with and he'd had butterflies in his stomach all morning. He told me that our manager's advice finally popped into his head and he decided to give it a try. He smiled and acted like he was calm and at ease and before he realized it he started becoming more at ease.

Start NOW: Use this time to get excited

Your perspective and mindset will make all the difference in helping your children adjust. And the adventure doesn't start on moving day, it starts now!

It's important to be honest with your children as you listen and support them when they share their fears and feelings. Like any new situation in life, it's also helpful to illustrate what the move will do for them. Paint a picture of the move in terms they'll understand. Describe the picture in a way that resonates with them and their life: a chance to meet new friends, to join a debate or hockey team that may not exist at their current school, to play in a new backyard with a swing set, or visit a great amusement park nearby. Get excited about it for them. Allow them to see and grab on to things they'll anticipate and look forward to. It doesn't change the situation, but it can adjust their frame of mind if you talk about the move in positive terms they can relate to.

Moving to a new location can be very exciting. There are new places to explore such as parks and museums, new things to try such as the local favorite food, and new opportunities for you and your children. It's easy to forget these aspects when you're anticipating the unknown. Instead of fearing change, invite your children to think of all the ways change has been fun in the past, like going to a camp, or remind them of great out-of-town vacations you've taken together. Have them think about other events in their lives that brought about changes, like each new school year, and discuss all the things they gained from those experiences.

Researching your new home and location is a great starting point. The more information you can give to your children, or allow them to discover for themselves, the more they'll start visualizing themselves in their soon-to-be home and begin to anticipate it. Do what you can to take them there in person (or in pictures) and do the rest via online research. Google Maps will allow you to see the new area down to street level. See Chapter 5 for more ideas on involving your children with their new city, home, or school.

If you can, take them house hunting or to the new area, show them the new neighborhood and visit places where your children will likely frequent (parks, school, etc.) where they can see children their own age. This will ease their anxiety by giving them more information and will add a fun forward-looking perspective that allows them to start planning and getting excited. Michelle, a friend of mine who moved around as a child, can still remember the excitement of house hunting with her parents. "Looking at new houses was the best. Each was different and fun, and I could start to imagine my life there as we'd walk through." If a trip isn't possible, once you've found a house, tell them their new address. Have them look up the location on a map and compare it with your current residence so they can get a broad picture of the move. Let your children get excited about picking their new rooms and how they want to decorate them (Do they want to keep the room the same or buy new bedding?). Talk with them about additional features the house has that they would be interested in (swing set, playroom, pool).

Other ways to help make the move more fun. Have your younger children envision someone whom they believe to be very brave. This could be a family member or friend, a character from a book or movie, or anyone really. Your children can picture themselves as a great adventurer taking on this new quest (i.e., Indiana Jones, Luke Skywalker, Dora the Explorer, or Harry Potter). When they're scared or worried they can picture themselves as their brave adventurer and think about what he or she would do. A colleague of mine had a son who loved Spiderman and would encourage him to think about Peter Parker/Spiderman in situations where he was nervous to summon up a bit more courage.

Providing your children with small treats can serve as a fun distraction as well. Within reason, let the children pick something they've been wanting. When my family left Chicago, my sister asked for a Chicago Bulls basketball jersey. You can also surprise and entertain them with something new during the move or to put in their new room on move-in day. My mom bought music and movies for our trip when we moved to Cincinnati. A small treat gives your children something to look forward to or serves as an unexpected surprise and distraction. Consider letting them do something special for the move (pick out new decorations or wall color for their room) or giving them something in the new house to make it more appealing. The promise of a new pet, a billiards or ping pong table, or a swimming pool can bring excitement to the move. The promise of a special treat will also involve your child in the process, which will be discussed in greater detail in Chapter 5.

It's a choice you make each day

In any situation, you ultimately choose how to respond and this is a great time to teach that important lesson to your children. This all may sound like overly simple advice, but viewing things as an adventure is an intentional decision and a daily choice. From time to time you may slip back into negative thinking and become frustrated, but don't get discouraged when you slip. Recognize it when it does happen, and correct it as soon as you notice it.

Each day is new and each day you can choose to face the situation as an adventure and an exciting opportunity. Don't focus on the past, don't fixate on the future, just live today and focus on making it a good day from sunrise until sunset. It will get easier with practice, as you remind yourself that even though you may not feel like it, you can take control of your thoughts and actions.

Although it can sometimes be hard work staying positive, it's actually not as hard as thinking negative thoughts, which take your time, energy, and efforts. Have you ever noticed how drained you are after a session of complaining or worrying? Why not direct that same energy into being positive? Practice optimism with your children and it may just become a habit over time.

Be aware of fatalistic thoughts and self-criticism. Being aware of those thoughts will help you change them. As you watch your own thoughts, model for your children how they can identify and share negative thoughts and make it a game to turn them into positive ones. Thoughts such as "I don't want to leave my friends; I'll never find friends I like as much as them," can be turned into, "I'm really lucky to have such great friends here, and I'll be sure to keep in touch. If really great people live here, I'm sure there will also be some great people who live in my new city. I'll create a plan for ways I can try to meet them". Also, as you work to banish your own negativity, teach them to banish the "I can't" thoughts in their head. Thinking about what they can't do or what won't happen is exhausting and depressing. Teach them to replace those words with optimistic words and remind them not to defeat themselves before they've even started!

To some degree it's not just your attitude about the move that's a choice; the decision to move itself is almost always a choice as well. You may not like the choice, but it's one which you and your spouse have deemed to be the best for your family. Remembering this will make you feel more in control. Your children may not have had a say in your decision, but you can show them they have the choice in how to respond to the move.

Your children will be affected by how you act toward the move

Try to refrain from excessive complaining or worrying about how much there is to do to prepare for the move. While understandable, this is a form of negative communication that can impact children when it's all they hear. There will be a lot to complain about, but for your children's sake (and your own sake), make the effort to not allow your worries and complaints to overwhelm the situation. Your children, at any age, will pick up on your attitude and it will set the stage for the move. Your attitude is a choice and that choice will have a much larger impact than you might realize. Not only will it help your personal transition, it will also help create a motivating and uplifting environment for your children and serve as a model for how to approach the changes and challenges of life.

Children learn in different ways. Some may be very open to direct advice about coping mechanisms, while others will be more receptive to observing how you handle things and then to trying them in their own lives without being directly instructed. I can remember overhearing a conversation while shopping one day where a young girl and her mom were arguing. The young girl was talking about how she hated having moved and exclaimed "I hate it and I know you hate it here too . . . you say so all the time!" While I don't know the specifics of their situation, it was clear to anyone within earshot that they both were unhappy, and I wondered to myself how much of the mother's own visible unhappiness impacted the attitude and efforts of her daughter.

It may not always feel like you're having an impact, especially with teens, but everyone benefits from being around positivity, even if their own mindset is negative at the time. Your children will continue to learn life doesn't happen to them; they're in control of their own mindset and how they choose to react to and handle the twists and turns along the way.

- A positive mindset is one of the most powerful tools at your disposal.

- Start NOW: Use this time to get excited.

- It's a choice you make each day.

- Your children will be affected by how you act toward the move.

Chapter 4: When Making Decisions, Put Yourself in Your Children's Shoes

"You never really understand a person until you consider things from his point of view... Until you climb inside of his skin and walk around in it."
— Harper Lee, <u>To Kill a Mockingbird</u>

Relocation is one of the major stress inducing events in our lives. This is especially true for families with children. To better understand how to help your children and family with the move, you'll need to take some time to think about how the move is personally impacting each of them.

Look at the world through your children's eyes

Childhood is a unique time in life. Almost everything is completely out of their control. As an adult, you're able to make decisions for yourself. If you want to buy something, you hop in the car, drive to the store and buy it. If you're considering a move, you deliberate over the pros and cons and then make your decision. But children have no control over their lives being turned upside down by a move. They didn't have a say in your decision and they can't do much, if anything, to change the situation. Keep in mind, your children are seeing this new journey in a whole different light.

Actively listening, asking questions, and giving them information and control when you can are suggestions which have been previously mentioned in this book and are all very important. Keep in mind, however, that each child is different. How they respond to the move, what their needs and concerns are, and how they'll handle the transition will differ. Try to understand how they're doing, how they're feeling, and how to respond to their concerns. Your youngest son might be very worried about the fate of the family pet. Your teenage daughter might be far more concerned about making new friends and how she'll fit in at the new school. Your assurances, planning, and communication should be focused on your children's world and their concerns.

Know your children

While you think through how your children will adjust to the move, here are some questions to consider:

What kind of student is your child? Is she currently doing well academically? Has she done well in the past and if so, under what circumstances? School size, class size, and different teaching techniques can play a role in your child's academic success. These characteristics can guide you in selecting the school which offers an environment where your child can thrive.

It's often easier to move children who are academically strong because they tend to find it easier to pick up on the new curriculum. They can then focus their energy on transitioning in other areas. That being said, if you know your child is struggling academically in one or more areas, make an effort to understand why. Look for tutoring options and visit the new teacher(s) to make them aware of your concerns.

How is your child socially? What's your child's personality? Is he prone to worry? Easy going? Extroverted or introverted? Knowing your children's tendencies will allow you to better understand what they'll face during the move. Those who are prone to anxiety will need more comfort and coaching than those who are easy going. Extroverts may have an easier time making friends than introverts, so be sensitive to an introvert's need to recharge by themselves at the end of a long day of meeting new people. Remember that introverts often find it more difficult to communicate their feelings, so look for different ways or mediums to help them process their emotions.

How is your child at making friends? Does it come easily or is it more of a challenge? If your children have easily made friends in the past, use those experiences to remind them there's no reason things shouldn't be the same in your new home and that they'll make good friends there as well. If one or more of your children has struggled making friends in the past, work on understanding what has limited them and try to give them advice for this move. Maybe they're shy and haven't been confident about smiling and making eye contact at first or have assumed others would approach them and so they didn't try to initiate friendships. Think of situations or events you could create that would allow your child to make friendships in a comfortable setting. See Chapter 16 for more on making friends.

How does your child react to guidance and advice? Your child may respond well to direct advice from you or may prefer to hear it from others. Your child may want to read the advice independently or listen to you talk through how you would approach things yourself and try to apply it to their own lives without being directly told to do so. Growing up, I responded well to advice when I requested it, but would bristle at unsolicited advice from my parents. They would adapt and find other ways to pass along meaningful lessons, often by relaying those very same lessons in stories they told me about their own day/experiences/worries. My sister, on the other hand, usually did not take advice well from me or my father but would always receive it well from my mother. Tailor the way you give advice to your children with how they prefer to receive and utilize it.

What does your child like to do for fun? Find a way to continue the activities your children enjoy in your new location. This will provide them with continuity, comfort, and a chance to make friends with similar interests. Research the requirements and deadlines ahead of time to ensure they can participate and inform them of the details so they have something to look forward to.

What matters most to your child at this point in life? Whether it's friends, school, family, sports, or hobbies, find out which things give your child the most joy, pain, or anxiety and focus your attention there. Keep in mind your child may be looking at the move as an opportunity for a fresh start; a chance to make changes in his or her life and try new things. There may even be some elements of the move which are appealing to your child. If your child was hanging out with the wrong crowd in school or was picked on by another student, this move could provide an escape from the situation and a chance for a new start. Talk with them about what changes they may want to make and create a plan to implement those changes.

Factor in your child's personality and hobbies when selecting when to move/start school

Determining when to move is often an aspect over which you have little control; however, there may be some elements which offer more flexibility. At the very minimum, you'll need to put some thought into the best time for your children to start at their new school.

Parents who move their children for the first time often believe, or have heard, they should move their children in the summer so they can finish the school year in one place. This would give them the entire summer to transition and then start their new school on the first day so they don't miss part of the new year. In my experience, and in the experience of others who I know, this isn't always the best time to move. It's worth taking all the alternatives into account before making your decision. Also, if you know of a school in the area you might be interested in, consider calling the school board ahead of time to check on their enrollment timing and policies (some school districts, especially private schools, may have restrictions that you will need to incorporate into your planning).

Be strategic in your decision. If your son or daughter struggles academically, beginning on the first day of the new year (or at mid-term) can minimize any disruption in his or her studies. If your child isn't struggling academically and doesn't need to begin at a specific time for sports or activities, social concerns should be considered. With those in mind, starting on the first day of the academic year may not be an ideal start date. On the first day back to school, the other students are less likely to notice your child or look out for them because they're too consumed with the excitement of seeing their friends and catching up on what they did over the summer. A new student will often fall through the cracks. If you're moving in the fall or summer, it may be better to wait a few weeks for the excitement to die down before starting your children. They won't miss much in terms of curriculum and will be more likely to be noticed by both the students and the teachers. Other students, once back to the normal grind, will be interested in reaching out to new students and more likely to offer them help.

As your children get older, their classmates sometimes become more insecure and less welcoming than those in elementary school. Your child may prefer to blend in by starting at a time when they're less likely to stick out and should be involved in this decision. This isn't a hard and fast rule; while many children and teens will appreciate their peers noticing and offering to help them, there are some children who will prefer to remain anonymous and their preferences should be taken in to account when possible. Walk them through the pros and cons of each option and solicit their thoughts.

If the move occurs during the summer, you won't have to disrupt your child's school year. However, unless you have activities to keep your child busy, summer can be a very lonely time to move. It may be harder for your children to meet friends in your new town as summer is usually when kids go to camp or vacation with their family. This creates a lot of alone time and your child may become bored or sad and miss their old friends. Without the benefit of being able to work on new friendships that will make their new home fun, your children will focus on their old home. It's human nature to miss what we have lost or don't have anymore. We're all more likely to become depressed when we're left alone with our own thoughts for too long and can't take action to make the situation better. If you do move in the summer, look into summer programs and camps in your new area to try to combat the isolation that can come with relocating when school is not in session.

My friend Emily's family moved early in the summer as she was preparing to enter ninth grade to ensure she was there in time for water polo tryouts. While the timing worked to ensure she could make the team for the upcoming school year, she still can remember the loneliness she felt for most of the summer as she sat around at home for the two months before the school year started.

For moves that occur later in the year, in some cases, it may be best for one spouse to stay behind with the children so they can finish the school year in their old school. However, if there's enough time left in the school year to make friends, it may work out well to move your children so they can begin to make friends and establish themselves in the new school. They'll then have a chance to make some connections for the summer and should feel more comfortable starting school the following year with a few familiar faces. The decision is up to you and your children and it's heavily dependent upon your unique situation (how much time is left in the year, how far you're moving, the age of your child).

You can't always control the timing of a move and sometimes there's no choice but to relocate during the middle of the school year. While, as previously stated, this may benefit the child, as teachers and students will look out for and help him or her, it can also create challenges with the curriculum. Because lessons are sometimes taught in a different order in each school district, the old school may not have gotten to a lesson that the new school has already covered. Your children would then miss that portion of their lessons. This doesn't always cause issues, but can lead to frustration and disappointment. If the course work is an essential building block for future work, you may need to get your children up to speed, either independently, with a tutor, or with your help.

If you have to move during the middle of the school year, consider taking the lessons and curriculum from the old school to the new one and meeting with the school administration to discuss any gaps. Consider resources like the Khan Academy for catch-up lessons from the comfort of your own home. While a mid-year move creates complications as classes and activities are in full swing, care, planning, and support will ease the transition.

Make sure younger children feel comfortable

When you're moving young children and toddlers, they'll need ongoing reassurance you're there for them. Usually their lives aren't as disrupted as when they're old enough to attend school. At this point, their world begins to center more around school and less on home and family. While friends aren't as critical to younger children as they are to teens, often their relationship with their new teacher is just as important. If your young child is old enough to attend school, see if they can meet their teacher ahead of time, and talk to the new principal about any mentor/buddy programs they have or could start. Contact the school psychologist to have him or her keep an eye on your child and schedule an occasional appointment to discuss any issues.

This younger group needs to feel safe, taken care of, and not forgotten. Establishing comfortable routines post-move and answering all their questions in a reassuring way will help ease their anxieties. It's also the chance to show them that although circumstances may change, they're still the same and they still have their family to rely on for love and support.

Moving with teenagers poses unique challenges

Teenagers are at a point in their lives where moving can be a much more emotional experience. It can sometimes take longer for them to adjust to a move than younger children and adults. Parenting a teenager can be challenging on a normal day; parenting a teenager through a move requires even more patience, understanding, and encouragement.

Teenagers spend a great deal of their time and energy finding, building, and maintaining friendships. Who their friends are, what groups they fit into, and who they're accepted by provide security and create the foundation for a teen's identity. When you tell them you're moving, they must leave all of this behind. Even more daunting is the idea that when they go someplace new they have to go through the arduous and awkward process of creating it all over again. This prospect can be frightening to teens and may provide some explanation for their reaction to the move (even if they haven't been able to articulate it themselves).

Additionally, teenagers are beginning to navigate into adulthood and crave independence while also needing security. When they're told they're moving and have no say in the matter, it's a jolting reminder they're not yet independent. However, keep in mind no matter how much teens want independence, they're also at a point where they still need the security of their family. They may talk and believe they can be on their own, but they still have some growing up to do and need their family's support and stability.

Remember, developmentally, teenagers have a lot going on mentally, physically, and emotionally, which is already causing them stress.

While all of these elements factor into why many teens take moving extremely hard, it's important to remember everyone's situation is unique. Some teens don't like their status in their current school's social structure and welcome a chance for a fresh start. Keep the lines of communication open and give them the space to react based on their own feelings and circumstances, and then meet them there to work on those feelings.

How can you best respond and help your teenager during the move? Let them feel heard and involve them. While this advice is repeated throughout this book for children of all ages, it particularly applies to teens. As teenagers are going through the emotional experience of thinking about losing their friends and their world, as they know it, they need to feel heard and understood. They need to feel their problems aren't being overlooked. Don't argue with them, don't try too hard to persuade them, and don't minimize what they're going through. This will make things worse.

Try to show them the bigger picture from the family's point of view. While teenagers are in a place where they think mostly of themselves, it does help to give them a broader perspective: why the move is occurring, how it will help or benefit your family, and how the other family members' lives will also be impacted. This should be done in a non-confrontational way which helps them understand. They may not react like they hear you, but they will be reminded they're not the only ones being affected by the move and that your family will need to support one another.

During one move in junior high my father gave me a bit more background on why he had taken a new job with a new company. Hearing the challenges at his former company (a boss whom he disagreed with and the limited career path that came from this conflict) and the thought process and struggles that he went through in deciding to take a new role and move his family gave me a lot more empathy for his choice. While still unhappy, I supported the move more as I realized that I would have made the same decision in his position.

As you begin to see things from their perspective and understand a bit of what's behind their reaction, continue to make yourself open and available for if, and when, your teen is ready to talk. Be prepared for emotional ups and downs. Your teen may be angry one day and quiet and withdrawn the next. He or she may be excited to start planning their new room in the morning and moody later in the day. Mixed feelings about the move are normal for everyone, but for teens, these ups and downs may be more pronounced and dramatic.

Watch for signs of depression. Most teens will experience sadness and loss during a move and while the process may be more emotional for them, they can make it through the transition successfully. Some teens, however, may suffer from depression during the process, which underscores the need to keep the lines of communication open. If you think your teen would benefit from speaking to someone, don't hesitate to seek professional help. Consider talking to the school's guidance counselor, or asking your family doctor for a recommendation. This book also contains a section on the grieving process in Chapter 12.

As with friends, academic and extracurricular activities take on a greater role as your child grows older and begins to think about applying to college. Treat your teenager like an adult when discussing their academic and school-related concerns (sports, social, etc.). It will help you to understand their apprehensions, make them feel cared for and respected, and give them a sense of control and independence. Begin by working together to best understand their needs and wants.

Whether they're on an advanced math track, in the orchestra, on the basketball team, or a member of the chess club, talk about the consequences of the move and begin to research schools in your new area to see what activities and options they have which align with your teenager's interests. Are they comparable or is there an alternative that will work? For instance, if the new school doesn't have a strong tennis team, is there a club nearby that excels in competitive tennis? If they've been on course to take advanced Mandarin classes, which no schools in the new area offer, are there nearby colleges, community centers, or online courses that offer international languages?

Also, consider any upcoming deadlines, events, tests, etc. at the current or new school which might affect the timing of the move. There may be some events (a major dance recital in two weeks) which would be helpful or meaningful for your teen to attend. This is also the time to consider the various options they have for schools in the area. Visit or research each school so that your teen can see alternatives and be involved in the selection process.

Moving is a fact of life and can be done in a way that doesn't hurt your teenager's ability to get into the college of his or her choice, but it's important to take steps to make sure class credits and GPA's transfer over accurately and that any conversions are reasonable. All school administrators are certain their school is more academically rigorous than other schools. Don't let them discount your child's past performance without justification. Each state creates its own standards, so consider the curriculum of the old school and new school and try to coordinate the two as best as possible.

Visit your current school's registrar for certified transcripts, as well as the school's course offering handbook. This will give your new school a reference point for placing your teen. Also, the schools may be on different schedules (semesters, quarters, block system, etc.) which may create additional problems. These difficulties aren't insurmountable, but they will require you to work with the school to help ease and coordinate the transition. While some credits and coursework may not directly transfer, it's important for your teenager to know you support their hard work. For more on transitioning to the new school see Chapter 15.

Additionally, you may want to consider having your teen ask his or her teachers for a letter of referral or a progress report detailing their efforts. Also, ask for a list of any relevant curriculum and textbooks, the learning style or approach used, and any special projects completed. This can help the teachers or counselors at the new school accurately place and instruct your teenager. If your teen is involved in any sports or clubs, he or she can have a former coach or advisor write a letter to the coach of the new program to help familiarize him or her with your teenager.

Moving during high school is hard but it can be done successfully and in a healthy way. Some teenagers may say they don't want to move with their family. Remember that they still need the support and love of their families and almost all of them will end up making the move, even though they will complain. However, moving at the end of high school can have social, academic, and emotional ramifications. My move in high school was definitely the most challenging of all my moves, but I was lucky enough to have it occur in my second year rather than my final year. If your family is moving during what is, or will be, your teenager's senior year of high school, it may be worth looking at different options and weighing the consequences of your teen moving or staying behind.

Should your teen stay behind? For many, senior year is a time for closure and finishing their high school career with friends whom they may have spent many years. If your teen does make the move, he or she won't have a lot of time to transition into the new school before heading to college, and it may be disruptive to the college application process. If your teenager is currently a senior, or entering senior year and wants to stay behind, talk with him or her and ask for his or her feelings about starting at the new school versus wrapping up senior year at the old one. In some cases, it may be better for your teenager to stay behind and finish out what is left of their high school experience and then join the family in the new location.

The decision really depends upon your family and your teen, the impact the move will have on him or her socially, developmentally, and academically, as well as on the options they have for staying behind. Some teens may or may not be developmentally ready to separate from the family; only you and your teen can decide what's best. If you feel your teen isn't ready, you can begin to think of creative options for minimizing the effects of the move based on what's most important to him or her at that time. Academic concerns are often a central factor in the decision to stay behind. Some schools differ greatly in credits and classes and a late high school transfer can significantly complicate matters.

My friend Katherine's brother made the decision not to move with their family during his senior year. He was able to stay with extended family and worked with his school district so that he could graduate early and thus only be separated from his family for six months rather than nine. Oftentimes creative solutions like this exist if you take the time to explore all available alternatives.

The most important thing is to find out how your teen feels and how the move could be made while minimizing the impact on his or her life. If your teenager insists upon exploring options to stay behind, work together to see if there are any viable alternatives. Are there relatives or a close and trusted friend who would have the means and be willing to host your teen? Will the current school district allow this to occur? Who pays for food and utilities? Will he or she have a car and a place to park or another means of transportation? What will be the house rules given your long distance relationship? Some teens will lose interest once all the logistics are laid out, but others may have a plan which you can begin to further investigate. Either way, it's a good exercise for older teens who are considering staying behind as it involves them in the process. They're more likely to be on board, either way, if they helped make the decision.

- Look at the world through your children's eyes.

- Know your children.

- Factor in your child's personality and hobbies when selecting when to move/start school.

- Make sure younger children feel comfortable.

- Moving with teenagers poses unique challenges.

Chapter 5: Involve Your Children in the Process as Much as Possible

"The circumstances of our lives actually matter less to our happiness than the sense of control we feel over our lives." — Rory Sutherland

"Tell me, I will forget. Show me, I may remember. Involve me, I will understand." — Chinese proverb

While moving puts children in a powerless situation, you can counteract some of that helplessness by letting them state their opinions, express their preferences, and be involved with each stage of the process. As long as you make it clear to them you'll take their opinion into consideration, even if you don't fully implement their suggestion, allowing your children to speak their mind will help them gain some semblance of control over the situation.

Any choices you can give them will help

Where you can, give your children the chance to have some say in their future. They're in a situation where their life is about to dramatically change and they have no control, so any decisions you let them make will help them feel involved in what's happening. Also, let them voice their opinions; don't assume you know what they want or are thinking. Give them a chance to be heard and they might surprise you. And even if you do know the answer, letting them voice their preferences gives them a chance to feel heard and valued.

No matter their age, your children want to feel included and empowered during this time of change and uncertainty. They want their preferences to be known and considered and to be able to say "yes" and "no" to some things. It may appear as if they're being rude or difficult, but try to remind yourself this is often a response to feeling helpless. Allow them to have a say in some things and let them know you'll make the effort to consider their input as you move forward.

Ways to involve your children:

-Goodbyes: who do they want to say goodbye to and how (would they like a party?)

-Their room: how would they like to decorate their new room

-The journey: what will they bring with them for entertainment during the move

-The house: what are their requests for your new home/neighborhood

-The move: are there any tasks they can help with in preparing for the move

-Activities: what activities would they like to continue or try out in your new town

-School: discuss their options and have them weigh in on what is most important

---

Involve them in house hunting

As you begin the house hunting process, ask them what features of the house, yard, and bedroom are most important to them. If

they're not sure of their preferences, tell them to think about their
current or previous house, yard, etc. and what they like and don't
like. My sister always wanted a yard with a good hill for sledding
during the winter and we both always requested a house with a
pool (although we usually did not get that wish granted).
Sometimes my parents were able to make our requests work, other
times they weren't, but we felt heard and reassured our opinions
mattered in the family and that they were looking out for us.

The extent you involve your children is up to you. While there are
many considerations in selecting a house that you may not want to
discuss in front of your children (commute, school district, resale
value, price, and other financial matters), try to involve your
children where possible. Whether you ask for their input before
house hunting, take them with you, bring home pictures of
options for them to look through, or take them for a pre-move
visit to your new home, it's important to involve them at some
stage of the process. Any level of involvement will give the
children more information, alleviate some of their anxiety, and let
them voice their opinions.

Encourage them to plan their new room/city/life

Once you've finalized your new living arrangements, encourage
your children to start thinking about and planning for their new
home. This, again, gives them some control over the process and
gets them excited for their upcoming adventure. Let them look at
a floor plan if possible. Have them choose their rooms and start
thinking about how they want to decorate them. They can even
sketch out a scale drawing with furniture of their new room so
they're prepared for move-in day! I have a friend who tried this
recently with her children and said that they were so excited to
layout their new rooms that they sat with graph paper and small
to-scale cut outs of their furniture for several afternoons, excitedly
assessing all of their options.

If they're old enough, have them research their new city and make a list of what they'd like to do when they get there. They can contact the local Chamber of Commerce and ask for information about the area, including parks, activities, calendar of events, etc., via a "relocation packet". Consider buying travel books about your new town for suggestions on activities and areas to explore. You can look up your new town (or the nearest city) online or on sites like TripAdvisor as well. Have your children look up their new time zone if you're moving to a new part of the country. This will allow them to start thinking about how and when to stay in contact with their friends.

Along with TripAdvisor and other travel and tourism sites, look up your town's website for information on:

- Community history
- Weather and climate
- Nearby attractions (amusement parks, ice rinks, malls, historic sites)
- Area landscapes (ocean, rivers, lakes, mountains, national parks, hiking trails)
- Local food and restaurants
- Clubs, organizations, and youth groups
- Sports teams and arenas/stadiums
- Museums and theaters

As mentioned earlier, one thing your children could potentially help make a decision about is their new school. If this is an option, involve them with your research. Ask them for feedback on the type of school they would prefer (public vs. private, large vs. small, walking to school vs. riding the bus). I always expressed a preference for attending smaller schools, whether it was private or public. For items to consider when selecting a school, see Chapter 6. If you've already selected a school, let them know where they'll be attending so they can look it up online. Pictures and information on hours, clubs, etc. will allow them to start looking forward to the transition and help them decide which activities they want to join. Once you've moved you'll still want to visit their school with them ahead of time so their first day isn't their first time seeing it. Conduct research online so they'll be able to view the school's website and search directory listings, or they can call the school directly to ask any questions.

Topics of interest to your children may include:

- Subjects and curriculum taught in their grade
- Bus schedules and routes
- Dress codes
- Grading policies and grading scale
- School and class size
- Start and end time
- Calendar (spring break, last day, first day, special holidays)
- Mascot
- School colors
- Lunch options
- Clubs and activities
- Sports (including any deadlines)

Contact the school to see if they can send a handbook or orientation packet and ask about the requirements for enrollment. If your child is receptive, he or she could email the school principal or guidance counselor and ask to be put in touch with one of the students for any additional questions (this way your child will already know a familiar and friendly face on the first day).

Think of ways for them to help

Your older children can also compile important information for the transition. If they have a part-time job they can ask their current boss for a letter of recommendation. If they work at a national chain store they can look into the possibility of transferring to a store in their new location. As discussed previously, they can also gather information on the curriculum at their current school to give their new school upon enrollment.

You can keep your children engaged with packing and preparations as well. Have them list or set aside the items they want to take with them on the trip versus items to be packed for the move. If you need help with cleaning or other preparations they can handle, give them the opportunity to help out in order to keep their mind from dwelling on the upcoming move. Even tasks as simple as making sure all the library books have been returned, or going through their belongings to select things to get rid of can help you and give your child the opportunity to be involved.

- **Any choices you can give them will help.**
- **Involve them in house hunting.**
- **Encourage them to plan their new room/city/life.**
- **Think of ways for them to help.**

Chapter 6: Choosing a House and Neighborhood

"Do what you can, with what you have, where you are." — *Theodore Roosevelt*

"Home is a name, a word, it is a strong one; stronger than magician ever spoke, or spirit ever answered to, in the strongest conjuration." — *Charles Dickens*

The process of moving is very hectic and unsettling, but you can help your children by making them feel safe, secure, and comfortable during this transition. Our home is often where we feel most comfortable, so selecting a home with that in mind will go a long way in helping your children adjust after the move.

Work on balancing everyone's needs

There are a variety of needs which must be balanced when selecting a place to live. Finding the right school district, neighborhood, house, price, and commute time is a challenging enough task and doing so on a rigid timeline adds yet another layer of stress. Given all that is going on, any preparations and research you can do before the house hunting trip will pay off during your search.

A primary concern for parents is finding a good school for their children. Wherever you move there will likely be both public and private options you'll want to research. If you know anyone in your new area, ask them for their thoughts and suggestions. Your realtor will also have valuable local insights. It's difficult to truly know the ins and outs of a place through internet research; asking locals for their thoughts will give you a much richer (though subjective) perspective. If you haven't yet found your desired school district, take the time to research your options so you know in which areas to begin your house hunting.

Questions to research or inquire about:

Financials: Cost of living, average price of homes in your area, taxes, and insurance rates.

Schools: Academic reputation of nearby schools (public and private), classes and extra-curricular activities offered, class size and estimated future growth of school (Is the school in a district where graduating classes are currently 300 but will increase to 1000 by the time your child graduates because there's so much new home construction in the area?), transportation options, tuition/books/fees (if private), programs for new students, and the process for transferring credits. Good sites to begin your search are: greatschools.net, publicschoolreview.com, privateschoolreview.com, and ecis.org.

Commute: You will want to know traffic patterns and possible routes to work from neighborhoods you're considering. As you consider your commute, check out Google Maps live traffic updates during rush hour for traffic patterns and delays to get a feel for the commute time from different parts of town. Drive the commute—it's worth your time. You may not have enough available time during your visit to drive it during rush hour, but make time to drive it at some point during your trip. Making this drive for the first time on your first day from your new home can be very stressful and surprising! If you will be moving to an area with public transportation, research the location (pick up and drop off), schedule, and price of each option and consider doing a trial run to test the amount of time the total commute will take.

Safety: Crime statistics in the area and surrounding areas.

The house hunting and selection process might need to take place within a very short time, sometimes just over a weekend. Expect a long, tiring weekend if this is the case. Try to do as much online research as you can ahead of time so you can make the most of your visit to the new location. Clearly think through your ideal wish list and prioritize the most important elements so you can factor them into your decision and find the right place for your family. Provide the list to your realtor to help guide him or her on how to make the most of your time. Be explicit about what you want, what you need, compromises you're willing to make, and ask a lot of questions so you feel comfortable with the area.

You may want to consider taking pictures of anything you want to remember for future reference. At the time, it may feel like you'll remember everything clearly, but once you're home, all of the houses will start to blur together and it will be hard to remember the specifics of any one house, room, yard, or location. Consider bringing a tape measure to record the dimensions of potentially hard to fit items (built-ins for a TV, a bedroom wall which will need to fit a large dresser and vanity). If you have time, visit or at least drive by the schools your children will attend. Like many things in life, something may seem good on paper, but looks entirely different when you see it in person.

Consider the pros and cons of temporary housing

When a move occurs, the timing is often fast and furious. You accept a new job and may need to be on site in a matter of days or weeks. There are a lot of unknowns. Temporary housing may be a necessary option depending upon the timing of the move. This can be beneficial in that it doesn't force you to rush to find a new place; you're able to take your time and make a thoughtful decision. My family's first move occurred when I was two and a half years old. We were in temporary housing for a month in a school district different from the one where we would eventually settle. For my parents, this worked well as I was too young for school or to notice much of my surroundings. Not having a permanent house gave my parents time to explore the area before we moved into our house and helped them feel a little more comfortable with things like shopping, doctors, church, and entertainment opportunities. By the time we moved into the house, they felt like they knew the area very well.

However, temporary housing often prolongs the transition time for older children as they're not truly able to start to settle in and "nest". The trailing spouse and children can potentially remain behind for a few weeks to orchestrate the move, or it may be necessary for everyone to be out of the old house and in the new city as soon as possible, for a variety of reasons. Either way, keep in mind the added stress temporary housing may cause and try to balance it out by introducing as many of your former routines as you can into your daily life to make things feel more familiar.

Minimize the time you're in limbo before establishing yourselves in your new home. Whether a condo, apartment, or house, home represents a constant and safe place to your children and allows them to form the attachment and connection they'll need once they begin to settle in.

I've known families who approach this in different ways, and the circumstances of your situation will be a crucial factor in your decision. One friend's family decided that the working spouse would go ahead and start work in the new city while my friend, who was in high school at the time, stayed behind with her mother and siblings to finish up classes for the semester (she was taking driver's education through her current high school and her new school did not offer this option, so she wanted to stay to complete the whole course). I had another friend whose entire family made the move immediately so that she could get established at her new school in time for swimming try-outs. In this case they felt that a quick move into temporary housing for six weeks in the new area and then taking their time selecting a house in that school district was the right decision for their family. There will be trade-offs either way, so the most important thing is to make an informed decision and work on balancing those trade-offs as much as possible.

- **Work on balancing everyone's needs.**
- **Consider the pros and cons of temporary housing.**

Chapter 7: Saying Goodbye

"Don't be dismayed at goodbyes, a farewell is necessary before you can meet again. And meeting again, after moments or lifetimes, is certain for those who are friends." — *Richard Bach*

"Some people come into our lives and quickly go. Some stay for awhile, leave footprints on our hearts, and we are never, ever the same." — *Flavia Weedn*

Taking time to say goodbye is important. Not everyone likes to say goodbye (goodbyes are sad!), but it's beneficial to see those people and places you and your children care about one last time. It will give your child and their friends a chance to find some closure.

Tell others when the news is final and the move is approaching

Growing up, I was often jealous of how lucky my friends were to be able to stay in one location while I had to move away. They didn't have to go anywhere; their lives stayed the same. Then, in the seventh grade, for the first time I had a good friend move away from me and I experienced the loss that comes with staying behind. She had to leave but would be going off to have fun, new experiences while my life would stay the same, albeit a little worse off now that a good friend would be gone. It was then that I realized both parties in the friendship suffer from a move. Be mindful of this fact when telling others, especially those you're close with, that you're leaving and try to put yourself in their shoes.

When you or your children tell friends and acquaintances about the move, odds are most will be sad to see you go but support your decision. There's always a small segment whose reaction will surprise you. I included my seventh grade story to remind you losing a friend to a move is also a loss for the friend staying behind. Based on the experiences which I and others close to me have had, I can tell you your friends may react to that loss differently than you would expect and in even ways which you may not find helpful at that moment. Be prepared for the following reactions: anger directed toward you, anger at your spouse/parents or whomever they believe "caused" the move, having an initial measured response but then cutting you off/out soon after hearing the news as they quickly try to minimize their own pain, or passive aggressive anger—saying they're supportive and sad but then making off-colored and unsupportive comments.

It's easy and natural to take these reactions personally and feel hurt and unfairly attacked, and it can really add to the stress and sadness of the impending move. It's important to remember all of these responses stem from their own hurt at being left behind. If you're close enough, your friendship will likely survive. Talk about it with your friends if you can. If either of you can't get past it, you need to move on. My moving experiences taught me that good friends always awaited me anywhere I went.

Remember that while it's important to share the news of your move with the people who are important to you, you may want to think twice about telling close friends and acquaintances early on or when things are still not finalized. I've made this mistake quite a few times. It's asking a lot of people to continue to treat you the same (at work, as friends, as members of a club or group) for months and months if the move is too far in the future. If you tell acquaintances too early, they sometimes begin to prematurely cut you out. Some may start planning for when you won't be there and give you less responsibilities at work or "forget" to invite you to social events. I hope this won't be the case for you, but it can happen from time to time. Tell close friends when you believe it most appropriate to do so and tell acquaintances once things are final and the time is approaching.

Take the time to say goodbye to both people and places that you'll miss

Goodbyes let your children hear from their friends that they're important and will be missed. This also gives your children the chance to give friends any notes or gifts to remember them by. Ask their friends to write them farewell wishes that they can read at their new home. Small gifts and notes from their friends remind them they can make new friends and that even if they haven't yet made them, and feel alone in the new city, there are people who still care for them in their old town. Don't be concerned that this tie to the past will hold your children back in the new place. It will give them strength by reminding them they're loved and that they did build past relationships that were important to them.

Remind your children that moving away doesn't mean the friendship is over. Even though they may not be physically close, they can stay connected if they choose to. If your children have been keeping a journal thus far, encourage them to write down their feelings about parting with friends. They can also write their memories down and chronicle all the good things they want to remember about the home and friends they'll be leaving.

The same is also true for adults and their friendships. There's no use in pretending you're not sad about leaving your friends and no good comes from avoiding it. Let your friends know they'll be missed, give them a chance to tell you the same, and make a plan to stay in touch.

Also, don't neglect to say goodbye to your favorite places. If there are places which have had significance in your life, or in your child's life, make one last visit to say goodbye in order to create one final memory of the time you spent there.

Create a closure plan

Ask your children how they would like to say goodbye, then help them make a plan to do so. A plan is important because it helps you use your time wisely. Are there friends you or they want to see a few times before leaving, or just once for some quality, one-on-one time? Remind your children their time is best spent enjoying their friends and not letting the stress erupt into bickering and fighting even though they both may have strong feelings about the move. Make a list of the people, places, and things you want to be sure to see or do before leaving. Ask your children to create their own list as well and then talk with them about the best way to go about checking names off the list.

Ask if they'd like to plan a party or get together with some of the people on their list so they can see them all at once. Although planning a party in the midst of a move may seem like unnecessary stress, children need to be able to see those whom they care about. If timing is tight, a party is a good way to say goodbye to a lot of people at one time. It is often less of a logistical headache than trying to make sure your child sees everyone individually, or leaving things to chance and having them be disappointed because they didn't get to say goodbye. The party can be as simple as a picnic or BBQ. We had several moves that coincided with Halloween, so my mom would host a Halloween party for me and my friends. It was a great excuse to see everyone before I left while still being more upbeat than a true "going away" party.

Alternatively, you can consider having the children invite over friends to help them pack! Some children may prefer spending the day engaging in their favorite activities with one or two good friends. They could have a sleepover, play video games, see a movie or attend a sporting event. The opportunity to say goodbye is what's most important. And don't forget to take pictures!

If you do decide to throw a party, in lieu of presents you can ask those attending to bring letters, photos, or mementos to add to a scrap book of memories for your children. Before one move in elementary school, we had a cooking birthday party and all of my friends came over one last time. We made breakfast together and each of my friends traced one of their hands on a white chef's apron and signed their names as a keepsake for me.

Other ideas include having guests sign or write notes in an autograph book, framing a group picture and having everyone sign the matting, or buying a personalize-able mug for guests to sign. When your child is in the new house and feeling a bit lonely, he or she can look at these mementos and remember the friends who care about him or her. Before one move, the girls on my soccer team signed a soccer ball for me to take with me. Before another, my friends and I bought lockets and had all of our initials engraved into them (in one long stream) so we would all be together as a group even when we were apart. I still have both of those items to this day and couldn't have asked for more meaningful parting gifts.

Additionally, ask your children if they want to also give their friends a note or small token of friendship to remember them. It could be anything from a framed photo or photo calendar to making them something which represents their friendship. If your child is artistic, he or she can create a comic strip or collage to give his or her friends. When I was in the third grade, my class took a field trip to a conservatory and we all bought plants. When we moved, I took cuttings from my plant and rooted them and gave my friends a plant to remember me by. As I got older, I'd write notes to the friends I was leaving to let them know how much their friendship meant to me.

If your child has one friend he or she is particularly close with, they could do something special together. They can create a video, make a photo collage or slideshow of their favorite memories, or buy matching items like stuffed animals. They could also easily create a scrapbook (or two!) that has photos and other mementos and reminders of their friendship and their favorite things so each of them has a book to remember the other by when they're far apart. Many online photo sites have very simple options to make nice photo albums. Make sure to have your children collect their friends' phone numbers and email and mailing addresses so they can stay in touch.

Goodbye Mementos *(have your children provide a gift to their friends or organize a gift for their friends to give to them):*

-Photo album or scrap book with pictures and letters from friends

-Framed picture with matting signed by friends

-Trinkets from your soon to be new home or from your favorite places at your current home

-Mug, pillowcase, t-shirt, or poster with friends' signatures

-Create a video or slideshow with photos and memories

Before packing, go through the house and take pictures or make a narrated video of all the rooms so you'll have them to look back on. It's amazing how quickly some memories can fade, even those you really want to remember. I often think back and wish I could remember what a specific house we lived in looked like. My parents still have video and pictures of most of the places we lived and although we don't look at them often, it's nice to have a record of memories. As you take pictures, you can also go room by room as a family and talk about your favorite moments in each. You can even make an album with pictures and stories from your old house to keep and look back on once you've moved.

You may feel alone, but keep in mind that you're beginning a new adventure

After you've told people about the move and started saying your goodbyes, you'll begin to feel disconnected. It can feel as if everyone else's life seems to be "full steam ahead" and you're in a state of limbo, just waiting to move. This can often cause people, especially children, to feel very disconnected and alone. This is entirely normal but not particularly fun. Remind your children (and yourself) that you're in transition and that you'll soon be in a new place and start to feel connected as you establish your new life there. Focus on things you're excited about (or which you can get excited about if you're not there already) and keep reminding yourself this time will pass.

When I think back to my moves, the first few weeks of transition left me with the most real and lasting feelings I can remember—particularly the period between saying goodbye and starting my new school. To sum it up, I wasn't always lonely, I wasn't always sad, and I wasn't always excited, but I almost always felt alone. When moving makes you or your children feel alone, any reminder this isn't the case and that you and they are in good company is a great comfort. Reaching out to others who've moved in the past can really help.

Additionally, talking about how the current move is personally affecting you can remind your children they're not alone. Reading books, blogs, or watching movies with a moving storyline is another great way to help you, your child, or your teen with the feelings of loneliness. It can also help your children process how they're feeling if they relate to the character who is also moving to a new city or school and in a similar situation and may be a safe way for them to express emotions and ask questions. It easily opens the door to a conversation about the characters and their worries, and then allows you to transition into talking to your child about their own worries. You can use the lists provided as a starting point to reference options and select the most appropriate for your child.

Younger Children

Books: Ages 3-8

- *The Berenstain Bears' Moving Day* by Stan Berenstain and Jan Berenstain

- *Alexander, Who's Not (Do You Hear Me? I Mean It!) Going to Move* by Judith Viorst, Ray Cruz and Robin Preiss Glasser

- *Who Will Be My Friends?* (Easy I Can Read Series) by Syd Hof

- *A Tiger Called Thomas* by Charlotte Zolotow and Diana Cain Bluthenthal

- *We're Moving* (First-Time Stories) by Heather Maisner and Kristina Stephenson

- *A Kiss Goodbye* by Audrey Penn and Barbara Leonard Gibson

- *Saying Good-Bye, Saying Hello...: When Your Family Is Moving* (Elf-Help Books for Kids) by Michaelene Mundy and R. W. Alley

- *Big Ernie's New Home: A Story for Young Children Who Are Moving* by Teresa Martin and Whitney Martin

- *Melanie Mouse's Moving Day* by Cyndy Szekeres

- *Elena's Big Move* by Sarah M. Olivieri

Books: Ages 8-12

- *Moving Day* (Allie Finkle's Rules for Girls, Book 1) by Meg Cabot

- *The New Girl* (Allie Finkle's Rules for Girls, Book 2) by Meg Cabot

- *The New Kid* by Mavis Jukes

- *Hey, New Kid!* (Puffin Chapters) by Betsy Duffey and Ellen Thompson

- *Moving Day (Katie Woo)* by Fran Manushkin and Tammie Lyon

- *Ellie McDoodle: New Kid in School* by Ruth McNally Barshaw

- *The Kid in the Red Jacket* by Barbara Park

- *Diary Of An Almost Cool Girl: My New School* - Book 1 by B Campbell and Katrina Kahler

- *The Year My Parents Ruined My Life* by Martha Freeman

- *Anastasia Again* by Lois Lowry

- *The Agony of Alice* by Phyllis Reynolds Naylor

Teens

Books: Ages 13+

- *Then Again, Maybe I Won't* by Judy Blume

- *Starring Sally J. Freedman as Herself* by Judy Blume

- *10 Dos & Don'ts When You're The New Kid: A Survival Guide for Teens Starting at a New School* by J.C. Tilton

- *Still Sucks to Be Me: The All-true Confessions of Mina Smith, Teen Vampire* by Kimberly Pauley

- *The Year My Life Went Down the Loo* by Katie Maxwell

- *Dear Teen Me: Authors Write Letters to Their Teen Selves (True Stories)* by Miranda Kenneally and E. Kristin Anderson

Movies*:

- *Clueless*

- *The Karate Kid*

- *10 Things I Hate About You*

- *High School Musical*

- *Harry Potter*

- *Footloose*

- *Twilight*

- *Cheaper by the Dozen*

- *Alice Upside Down*

- *Mean Girls*

* Content may not be age-appropriate for all children. See individual ratings.

Moving may occur for different reasons and is a uniquely individual experience, but some of the key tenets to adjusting and establishing your new life are the same no matter your age or location.

- **Tell others when the news is final and the move is approaching.**
- **Take the time to say goodbye to both people and places that you'll miss.**
- **Create a closure plan.**
- **You may feel alone, but keep in mind that you're beginning a new adventure.**

Part II: Preparation and Moving Day

Chapter 8: Preparing for the Move

"A good plan is like a road map. It shows the final destination and usually marks the best way to get there. . ." — H. Stanley Judd

As the move draws near, your to-do list will grow (planning, cleaning, packing, goodbyes, tying up loose ends, etc.). Stay as organized as you can, and don't let the stress of the move overwhelm you.

Logistics: plan ahead and make lists

There are a lot of details to remember when preparing for a move. Make a list so you can be sure you won't forget anything. If there are things on the list your children can help with, assign them a task or two. This gives them a chance to feel in control and will keep them busy and their minds off the upcoming move. As you send your change of address notices to magazines, banks, friends, and family, if your child is young, include their friends' parents on this list. You might also give your child the chance to send out their own change of address notes. They can send letters, postcards, emails, or texts. The choice is theirs (and of course, caution them about posting specific and private details on social media).

As you check off items on your to-do list, the move is a chance for you to teach your children how to manage their time and resources when so much needs to be done in such a short time frame. Show them your lists which you've broken into separate segments and timelines. Point out how you've selected the most important things to focus on and that other things may not get done (e.g., we have to return the library books and get an oil change for the drive so we may not get the chance to dry clean items before packing them). Help them to understand that when a lot needs to be done in a short period of time, it helps to break the larger tasks into smaller items to make them more manageable and less overwhelming.

If you're selling your home, there are a few logistics to keep in mind. I learned a lot from my family's moves in terms of the psychology of sales when getting ready to sell our homes. Making everything neutral is key so as to appeal to (or rather, so as not to offend) a variety of tastes rather than just those who share your style. Taking down as many photographs as you can so the new buyer doesn't see it as your home but starts to envision it as their own will help improve "saleability". Making the home as clean and clutter free as possible goes a long way toward helping sell your home. Many people become distracted by what may appear to be minor things. Even in the midst of the stressful or the mundane, your children can learn as you work to prepare the family for the move. Your realtor will help guide you through this process, but let it serve as a reminder that opportunities exist even in the most unexpected areas to help teach your children life skills.

If your family has pets, extra consideration and planning up front should be spent in preparing them for the move. If you have any concerns, talk to your veterinarian about how to best prepare for moving your pet. Pets are often like members of the family, so if you're able to move them with you it will prove to be a welcome source of comfort and familiarity for the children.

If you have to leave the pet behind, give your children time to say goodbye and realize they may view this pet as a member of the family or a close friend, which will be yet another loss to them.

Work to find the pet a good home with neighbors, family, or friends, or see if those you know may know of others who would be glad to take the pet into their home.

Make sure to set aside items to take with you

There'll be items you won't want to pack and move in the truck but will want to keep with you (valuables, important paperwork, anything irreplaceable such as one of a kind mementos or heirlooms). Your children will also want to think about what they want to have with them. For children, moving introduces a lot of newness all at once so it will be important to have familiar and comforting things with them (a teddy bear, favorite book, pictures, music to listen to).

Have your children set aside a backpack or tote which won't be packed, and have them select some items they want to carry with them during the move. Tell them to keep their bag with them or designate a place where the bags will all go on moving day to ensure they don't accidentally get loaded on the truck. Also, place any necessities in the bag such as toothpaste, pajamas, or clothes. There was one move where my mother left a stack of bills to be paid on the kitchen counter, went out to run an errand while boxes were being packed, got back and found the bills gone. She had to go through four boxes to find them. Save yourself the stress and carefully set aside what you need!

Put information related to your child's textbooks, transcripts, and curriculum, which they will need at the new school, in an easily accessible spot. Schools require proof of immunizations for enrollment. Be sure to set those documents aside so they're readily accessible when you enroll your children in their new school.

Think of what will make the journey more fun and set aside those items to take with you. Ask if one of the children wants to make a playlist for the drive or flight for themselves or for the entire family to listen to. Set aside snacks or games for the trip as well as books and magazines to read. Consider packing some special surprises for them for the day of the move (or for the trip) to keep them entertained as well as adding an element of excitement to the day.

Pack ahead of time

Packing is a great opportunity for "spring cleaning." It forces you to go through all of your belongings and get rid of things you no longer need or use. The more you get rid of, the less you'll have to pack, move, and then unpack! Sort through your clothes, household items, etc. and have the children do the same. Make piles for donation, trash, friends, and family (Done with those baby clothes? Give them to a neighbor who just had a baby!).

If you want to sell your items, a garage sale is a great way to get your children involved (making signs, price tags, etc.), and they may be excited to make some extra money for the move. You can also use sites like eBay or Craig's List to sell items. Have your children help you establish a price for each item. Your children can learn a lot from watching what sells and what doesn't. Have them establish a "price to sell" approach. They can get an idea of what's reasonable by searching prices of similar items on eBay. Have them keep a log of what you've sold and at what price.

If you want to have a garage sale, plan the day and time and set up signs around your neighborhood to guide people to your home on the day of the sale, or team up with your neighbors to have a joint garage sale. Be willing to negotiate! People come to garage sales expecting to bargain, so don't be surprised or insulted when they try to get a lower price. Try to negotiate a fair price, especially later in the day when you want to get rid of your sale items (consider donating those you don't sell). Throughout the process, take pictures of any item you can't or won't be bringing with you which has special meaning and which you want to remember. Someday you may want to remember what your child's first bike looked like.

Will you be packing yourself? Different companies and organizations offer different options for relocation. If you're packing yourself, start as early as possible on those items you won't need to use over the coming weeks. Packing almost always takes significantly more time than people expect and you don't want to add unnecessary last minute stress to an already stressful situation. There are a variety of ways to get boxes: reach out to anyone who has recently moved to see if they still have their boxes, try Craig's List/freecycle.org postings, or you can ask grocery stores and big box stores like Wal-Mart, liquor stores, bookstores, or home and hardware stores. Having matching or similar sized boxes will make stacking them substantially easier. Additionally, U-Haul has a customer box exchange, or you can buy boxes online and have them shipped to you. Moving companies usually sell new and used boxes as well as packing paper. Some types of boxes and moving materials (mattress bags, wardrobe boxes) may be harder to find and you may need to purchase these for the safety of your items and to efficiently pack and make use of space.

Remember to carefully wrap and cushion breakables as you pack items and label the breakable boxes "Fragile" so whoever picks them up knows to handle them with care. As you prepare for the move, collect and save any bubble wrap or packing peanuts you come across. Newspaper makes a great, cheap wrapping material, although the print may rub off so be selective in the items you wrap. Paper towels also work, but packing paper is inexpensive and probably the most effective. Use old blankets and towels or buy/rent pads for nice furniture. Try to keep all pieces and their accessories together if possible. Take bolts and screws out of dressers and tape them in one of the drawers. Use small plastic food storage bags to keep the pieces together. Keep cords wrapped with the appropriate electronics. You may think now that you'll remember where you put them, but when you're unpacking you'll likely have forgotten.

Take the time to label the contents of the boxes and mark the sides so they can be easily read when stacked. This will help you determine which room to place the boxes and you'll know what's in each box. Avoid the temptation, as tiredness is setting in, to just default to "Misc." for each box. You'll really appreciate you made that extra effort later. The only labeling exception is for valuables. If you're not moving everything yourself, remember to think twice before labeling boxes as "jewelry" or any of your electronics such as an Xbox or other valuables; you don't want to alert others this would be a good box to steal. While most movers are trustworthy, it's better not to tempt fate and call out valuables. Ideally, you should keep your valuables with you, but for larger items this may not be possible. A simple pre-determined label you can remember or a symbol ("Files" or "@") will suffice to remind you the contents of the box are valuable while not alerting others.

If your children are old enough to help, give them a quick tutorial (heavy items on the bottom, not too many heavy items in one box, don't over-pack a box so it's busting at the seams) and then have them help pack up their room. This way they'll know how to access their things when they get to the new house.

Finally, keep the items you need for everyday use until the final day of packing and make sure they're easily accessible when you arrive at your new home.

Select the best moving option for your situation

If you're moving yourself there are a variety of options. One great option, if you believe you may need to keep your things in storage for a week or more, is a portable storage unit (Pods or Door-to-Door Storage). These are self-contained units which are dropped off at your house. You can pack at your leisure and when finished, the company picks them up and can either ship them to your new location or hold them in storage until you're ready for them to be shipped.

If you're moving directly from your current home to your new home you can rent a truck (U-Haul) or hire movers to handle the driving for you. If you don't mind driving yourself but would like some help moving the heavy items onto the truck, there are many services available such as hireahelper.com. You can search online for the various services and check ratings and reviews. The primary benefit of a DIY approach is clearly in the savings. Hiring movers is a bit more costly but eliminates a lot of heavy lifting and stress and allows you to focus your attention elsewhere. In order to get full insurance coverage on items lost or broken, you may need to have the same service pack, load, and move you, so be sure to check on this and weigh it into your decision as you finalize your moving plans.

- **Logistics: plan ahead and make lists.**
- **Make sure to set aside items to take with you.**
- **Pack ahead of time.**
- **Select the best moving option for your situation.**

Chapter 9: Moving Day

"When one door of happiness closes, another opens; but often we look so long at the closed door that we do not see the one which has been opened for us."
— *Helen Keller*

The big day is finally here. . . .

Everyone has a role

On moving day, there'll be a lot going on: last minute packing, organizing movers, people going in and out. It will be stressful, so talk to your children ahead of time and decide whether they'll be there and if so, the best role for them to play. Would you rather they went to play at a friend or neighbor's house? Do you need them to help with last minute packing, labeling boxes, the move itself, or do you need them there but to stay out of the way of the movers? Do you want them to help you clean the house as boxes are being carried out? Decide ahead of time what's preferable for both you and your children so you have a plan worked out for when moving day comes. Additionally, you might consider hiring a sitter for moving day if no friends are available to help.

If your children will be at home during the move, oftentimes helping out and getting involved will distract them from the more painful parts of watching their world become disassembled. If the move and work is being handled already, have activities they can do or a place they can sit.

Remember to buy your movers (professionals, friends, family, anyone really) lunch, snacks, and cold drinks. Whether they're being paid or not, this will go a long way in making those who are handling your personal belongings feel appreciated and will help to ensure your belongings are treated well. You'd be surprised at how many people overlook this and how appreciative movers can be when you think about them. Remember to tip; although it's not mandatory and up to the customer, if you feel like your stuff has been treated well, 5% of the moving cost is typically suggested.

Emotions may run high on moving day

Moving day (move-out and move-in) will be a stressful time. Keep in mind tensions may be running high and people will be on edge. Your children may find it unsettling to watch all of your family's possessions being loaded into a van and taken away. Assure them their belongings and furniture will be transported safely to the new house and that they'll see it all again once you arrive at your new home. Check in with them throughout the day to see how they're doing. Sometimes it's really exciting to watch a move happen, and sometimes it's really sad watching your home turn into an empty house you're about to leave.

Make it a game. I've found a great way to get through tough, boring, or stressful situations is often to try to make a game out of it. My sister and I used to play hide and seek and make our own makeshift mazes or forts out of the boxes in different rooms which hadn't yet been emptied. As the boxes were being moved inside we would try to guess which room they'd be taken to before we saw the label to see how many we could guess correctly. Today when I ask her about her memories of moving, those games are one of the first things she mentions. After the house has been emptied, have everyone do a final check to see if you've missed anything. Once the logistical part is over, for anyone who wants to, do a final walkthrough and say goodbye.

Pack entertainment for the journey

Road trip! Whether flying or driving, you're off to your next destination, and like any other trip, it's a good idea to take things for your children to entertain themselves with and have snacks prepared, depending upon the length of the trip, as well as any necessities. Teens and older children probably won't have trouble entertaining themselves, but the key for all age groups is to think ahead and make sure everyone is setting aside items they'll want for the trip so they don't get packed on the truck.

For car trips, classic road trip games are sometimes a great option, especially for younger children. Try to find all the states on license plates, or all the letters or numbers up to 100 on signs and billboards. Listening to good music can also get you a long way. Follow your progress on a map so the children can see where and how far they've traveled.

- **Everyone has a role.**
- **Emotions may run high on moving day.**
- **Pack entertainment for the journey.**

Chapter 10: Moving In

"We are made to persist. That's how we find out who we are." — *Tobias Wolf*

"Home" is a powerful word. It can mean something different to everyone, but ultimately it means a place where you feel totally comfortable. Home is where you don't have to try, worry, or put in extra effort to fit in. You feel relaxed and you belong. And today you're on your way to settling into your new home.

If temporary housing is your next stop, work to make it feel like home

You may not be able to move into your new residence directly and instead require temporary housing (a motel, extended stay hotel, or corporate housing) for a few weeks or months. As mentioned previously, this is often necessary but can be tiring as not being able to start the full settling in process can prolong the transition.

If you find yourselves in temporary housing, make the best of it. Remind everyone to be grateful for a roof over your head and for being together. Try to make it feel a bit more like home during your stay by placing small pictures or photos on tables and bringing your "comfort" items with you (a cozy blanket, a favorite journal, or notepad). Unpack your temporary items and put your things in drawers or closets if available. Don't live out of suitcases if you can help it! Take the time to explore the area and play with your children—continually choose to make it an adventure. To minimize the time we would spend in temporary housing, my mother, sister, and I would often stay behind in our house while my father went ahead to start work. But during several moves we did spend some time in temporary housing and my sister and I would enjoy playing in the hotel pool or in their arcade and game room.

Waiting to move into your house means putting some things on hold (completely unpacking, etc.), and it can make the children feel like other things need to be put on hold as well, like getting to know the area, making friends, or joining clubs and activities. Don't allow your temporary status to keep your family from starting to connect with people and places in the area. Encourage your children to get involved in activities and start reaching out and making friends.

Make the most of move-in day

Move-in day is often more exciting than move-out day. The children will get to see all of their things again, and you begin the process of settling into your new home.

We'll cover unpacking in more depth in the next section, but as was the case for move-out day, you'll want to give your children things to do to keep them busy. If they're old enough, have them help direct where they want their furniture and then start to unpack their room. This assures them their things will go where they want them to go, keeps them busy, and allows them to see their belongings and surround themselves with familiar things. Unpacking can be a lot of fun for children. Occasionally they will unpack items they forgot they owned. The process of re-discovery is almost like getting it new again!

The first night in the new house can be sad. It won't feel like home yet and you'll have a lot of boxes everywhere with bare walls and minimal lighting. Try to unpack a few items to make it more comfortable (lamp, towels, stuffed animals for the children). It will also help to plan a fun activity or have something for the children or family to do (books to read, games to play, going out to dinner, etc.) for the evening. One interesting idea I've heard is that many kids love the fun and adventure of a camp out. You can consider making the night a "camping" night where you all sleep in sleeping bags inside on the family room floor. Make it a fun game and the house won't feel as empty anymore.

The first morning may also be a bit unsettling. You (or the children) may temporarily forget where you are. Waking up in the middle of the night to get a drink of water can really be disconcerting as well! Keep reminding yourself and your children that even though it doesn't seem like it right now, it will soon feel like home. The good news is it starts right from move-in day; you'll feel more at home each day from then on!

- **If temporary housing is your next stop, work to make it feel like home.**

- **Make the most of move-in day.**

Part III: Settling In After the Move

Chapter 11: Unpacking and Exploring

"The secret of change is to focus all of your energy, not on fighting the old, but on building the new." — Socrates

The movers have come and gone. You're in your new home and your new city. Now what? The key is to get back to normal as quickly as possible, make it feel like home, and return to old routines and develop new ones. It's hectic to do this at first, but it's very important to the settling in process.

Let the children unpack their rooms

If they're old enough, let the children take responsibility for unpacking and settling into their rooms. Along with keeping them busy this will give them some control of the situation by making decisions for themselves. It will also help them feel more at home. Help them with their decorating decisions. Remind them to look for outlet and light switch locations as they're telling the movers where to put their furniture and help them determine the best layout so they can start unpacking their boxes as soon as all of their furniture has been moved in. Although you may have plans to paint or want to rearrange things, try to balance those initial concerns with getting your children unpacked and surrounded with their belongings so their rooms feels like home as soon as possible. You can always cover things up to protect them when you paint or move furniture around later. It's far more important to help ease the children's transition those first few days in the new house.

Give your children the chance to personalize their room in their own style and with what makes them happy. Your children can decide if they want their new room to feel like their old one or try something new. They may crave consistency or relish the chance to experiment and be creative with new ideas (either in layout or decorations). If your children initially want to dramatically change the look of their rooms, make sure they keep some familiar items so once the excitement dies down they're not overwhelmed with everything feeling new and out of place.

Unpack quickly—the sooner you're unpacked, the sooner things start to feel like home

Preferences on unpacking vary. Most of us know people who still have boxes that need to be unpacked years after a move. My family was at the opposite extreme. We felt the boxes just reminded us of the move and took away from the settled in feeling, so our goal was to unpack the boxes within the first few days. That didn't mean having our things totally organized; we would unpack and pile up the boxes in the garage or have them hauled away so we didn't have to see them. We would often put our stuff in piles or stack it precariously on a cluttered bookshelf as we decided where to permanently put things. This is actually helpful in a number of ways. Your children may feel more at home seeing their familiar belongings. This also allows them to think through their options (throw it away, put it where it always was, place it in a new setting). They may also see the piles and feel compelled to put things away just to get rid of the clutter. It was often a hectic and tiring ordeal to unpack all the boxes early on, but I wouldn't have done it any other way.

Your environment can have a subconscious impact on how you feel. Make it feel like home so it isn't depressing. Take breaks when you need to, so as not to burn yourselves out. Focus on settling in and making the house a home as quickly as you can. You won't feel settled in the new location if you're not comfortable in your house. That being said, each family should determine what works best for their situation.

Along these same lines, after the unpacking and organizing is nearing completion (and you want to throw yourself on the couch and sleep for a week!), take the opportunity to lay out pictures and wall décor and decide where you want to hang some or all of it. Nothing says "we just moved in and aren't settled yet" like empty walls. The sooner you can get something, anything, hung up, the sooner the environment will feel lived in. Even if you're not ready to put up everything and want to take time to think through new decorating options, put a few items up (especially family pictures) in places where you know you want them. If you change your mind, the worse that can happen is you end up moving the picture and spackling a small hole. This will go a long way in making your house your home.

You need to make the most out of every home. Fix it so it becomes yours, even if you're thinking of moving again. It will make your time there more comfortable and thus is worth the effort. The next thing you know you'll be saying, "I feel like I've been here forever" and can't imagine ever leaving.

Encourage the children to explore the house, yard, and neighborhood

As your children get settled into their rooms during the first week, encourage them to explore the yard and neighborhood. Exploring will continue to make the move feel like an adventure. You can go on a walk with them to look for other children in the neighborhood (or for indications children live nearby like swing sets, cars with local school decals, or toys/bikes in the yard). If anyone is outside, introduce yourselves. Don't wait for others to approach you! Sometimes people don't know what to say to new people or they're shy, so you should take the initiative and introduce yourself and encourage your children to do the same thing (in the neighborhood and throughout the move).

If the neighbors aren't out, over the next few weeks drop by their homes and quickly introduce yourself. It can be as simple as, "Hi, just wanted to say hello and introduce myself. I'm Jane Smith and we have just moved in down the street at 123 Maple Blvd." You can ask if they have children and let them know your children's names and ages so the neighbors are aware and watching out for them. A simple five minute visit may feel awkward at first but will help you get to know your immediate neighbors and may potentially help the children meet friends nearby. It also shows your children how to take initiative, be sociable and conversational, and make friends.

Another activity for children is to map out the neighborhood and surrounding areas and mark where their house and other important landmarks (school, parks, etc.) are located. This will help them get their bearings. Also, make sure your children have their new address written or recorded somewhere.

Get to know your new area

In the first weeks, find the post office, grocery store, gas station, etc. closest to you. Finding these things, even if they don't end up being where you regularly go six months from now, is still immensely helpful. You will feel out of place and lost at first, so each place you're able to find and feel comfortable navigating to will help you feel more in control in your environment.

All of this has been made much easier through technological advances. Now you can simply push a button on your smart phone or computer and find out where you're going and what's in your surrounding vicinity. This is very helpful but not sufficient. Nothing can replace actually driving to the places nearby to see them yourself. You may have heard of things around you, but until you actually experience seeing them yourself you may not truly feel like you have an awareness of your surroundings. Drive around with your family and see what parks, restaurants, and fun places are nearby as well.

There are certain things you'll want to do quickly and others that can wait. Finding a doctor, dentist, and bank (and potentially a place of religious worship) will likely top your list. Other things, like finding a hair dresser or mechanic or getting an in-state driver's license and plates will follow the more immediate needs. Along with word of mouth and asking those you meet for their recommendations, there are some online resources available to help you in your healthcare search. Take a look at sites like Vitals.com and HealthGrades.com to see if any doctors and dentists in your area have received reviews. For a starter list, see Appendix II.

- **Let the children unpack their rooms.**
- **Unpack quickly—the sooner you're unpacked, the sooner things start to feel like home.**
- **Encourage the children to explore the house, yard, and neighborhood.**
- **Get to know your new area.**

Chapter 12: Moving is an Emotional Time

"The greatest discovery of my generation is that man can alter his life simply by altering his attitude of mind." — William James

When moving to a new environment, new feelings may emerge. Before the move, the new house was a future idea, now it's a present reality. Children who may have felt excited before may suddenly feel sad and lonely and those who were dreading the move may be excited once they see the new house but frustrated they don't yet feel settled. No matter what's going on, recognize this change may bring about some new feelings or intensify existing ones in your children. Check in with your children, encourage them, hug them, remind them soon it will feel like home and listen to their fears and concerns so they feel heard.

Talk about it—worries and fears are less powerful when spoken out loud

There is power in sharing your fears and getting them out of your head—you can take some control in figuring out ways to address them. The fear built up in our minds is almost always worse than reality. Expressing these fears out loud puts them into perspective and lessens the hold they have over us. Ask your children what worries they have, just as you did before the move.

Now that they've moved and their first day of school is looming, more concerns are likely to arise. Assure your children it's normal to have concerns about making friends, fitting in, navigating their way around, and academics and classes. Have them write down a list of new worries and questions you can address or research. They may wonder about what the other children will wear. Clothing which was popular at the old school can sometimes make them feel out of place at the new school. A friend of my father still has a vivid memory of arriving at his new school wearing a shirt that was perfect for his old school but made him feel like he had the word "loser" on his back for his first full day at the new school.

My friend Andrea can vividly remember moving from Miami to NYC. Her brother went to school the first day dressed in shorts and a t-shirt and was so embarrassed that he called their mother to have her pick him up early! Try to visit the school before your children's first day to get a feel for what clothing and accessories will make them feel comfortable. They may also worry about lunch. Call the school to ask about lunch time, food options, and if seating is assigned.

Once again, keep communicating. Don't assume that just because your child hasn't brought things to you that he or she isn't struggling. As you did before, ask questions and touch base periodically. If your child is not sharing with you, suggest speaking with the school guidance counselor, coach, teachers, religious leaders, friends, or other family members. Encourage your child to continue to journal. New things will come up as they adjust and a journal is a good way to process how they're feeling over time.

Understand the grieving process

You're likely familiar with the five stages of grieving. Relocation often means leaving behind friends and comfort. If you've left family behind (grandparents, aunts, uncles, cousins), the transition can be even more challenging. Everyone grieves loss differently. You and your children may go through one or more of these stages: denial, anger, bargaining, depression, and acceptance. The American Academy of Child and Adolescent Psychiatry states that, "Moving to a new community may be one of the most stress-producing experiences a family faces."[1] Recognizing that they are grieving from a loss and preparing for possible reactions from your children will ease the process.

Denial. Before the move your children may have hoped you would change your mind, that the move would fall through and they would get to stay where they were, or felt if they didn't cooperate maybe the move wouldn't take place.

Anger. Your child may be angry with you and try to punish you for the move. When I had to move in the middle of high school, I recall trying to think of ways to punish my parents. I didn't blame them for the move; I knew how badly they felt about moving me, but I was really angry and wanted to take that anger out on someone. I can remember being intentionally difficult to please and picking fights just for the sake of being contrary because I had this anger welling up in me that needed to be released.

Bargaining. Your child may try to think of solutions to problems so the family move won't take place. I've heard from a few moms whose children promised to behave better, as if the move was a punishment for past transgressions.

Depression. After a move, I would usually cry and feel saddest before going to bed each night for the first few weeks. The tiredness from a day of taking on the unfamiliar would suddenly weigh down on me, and I would cry and tell my parents how

---

[1] The American Academy of Child and Adolescent Psychiatry (AACAP) Children And Family Moves No. 14; Updated March 2011.

much I hated the new school/city and beg to go back to my old home.

My sister would approach things entirely differently than I would. She was rarely, if ever, vocal about the pain she was in (even though she likely felt pain and discomfort for a longer time than I did because she takes longer to adjust to change). Although she wasn't as vocal throughout the process, she was grieving and adjusting in her own unique way. Your children will have their own way of transitioning—there is no set formula.

Watching and dealing with your child's anger or depression is difficult. Seeing your children in pain can be equally painful for you, but it's important that you allow them to go through these stages and express their emotions in healthy ways. Don't tell them they're wrong or silly for being angry or bargaining; listen to them, love them, and support them. Let them know you hear and understand them and help them get through these stages so they can eventually move on to acceptance.

Continue to listen and support

Each child is different and will struggle in different areas. As mentioned earlier in Chapter 2, if you or your child feel that talking and giving the move time isn't working, take action and get your child professional help as soon as possible. After the move, continue to watch for: a general lack of purpose or excitement for the future, things that used to make them happy no longer bring them joy, they cannot shake the general feeling of sadness, or they have changes in sleep, appetite, or energy levels.

Moving is one of life's biggest stress inducers and professionals, like counselors and psychologists, are specially trained to help you and your family work through these tough times. Again, if a move is happening along with other difficult family problems (financial issues, divorce, death), this can exacerbate the situation and make coping more challenging for your child. Short-term help and counseling can be a good way to get your child the support they need. Don't hesitate to seek out resources that can help.

Resentment can emerge very quickly in a move. Remember, as parents, it's vital for you and your spouse to be a team and support one another. Be open with one another about how you're doing and what you need. Communicate early and often so you can approach the move continually as a team and be there to support your children as well.

Spend time together

Spending time together is important, even if your children don't want to talk about things directly. It shows them you're there for them, they're supported and not alone, and it can help you assess how they're doing. They're going through a time of change and they need security, comfort, and love. Whether your children are toddlers or teens, they still want to know and see that they are loved. Try to set aside time to "hang out" and grab ice cream. Make the most of the moments you already have together: dinner time, time in the car, or bedtime.

If you're looking for additional ways to spend time together, take an interest in what they like to do. Whether it's watching sports, TV shows or movies, reading books, or watching the activities they participate in, share an interest in their world and you'll have more to talk about with them.

- Talk about it—worries and fears are less powerful when spoken out loud.

- Understand the grieving process.

- Continue to listen and support.

- Spend time together.

Chapter 13: Expectations

"Our greatest glory is not in never failing, but in rising up every time we fail."
— *Ralph Waldo Emerson*

How do you feel about surprises? A surprise birthday party? Perhaps. A surprise on your credit card bill? Probably not. And in general, when entering new situations, most people prefer to know what to expect. Whether the news is good or bad, highly likely or only a possibility, knowing what to expect can be empowering. It directs your energy toward addressing the situation rather than toward worrying about it. You can't be prepared for everything (nor do you want to exhaust yourself by trying!), but it's a good idea to get a feel for what you can potentially expect.

Setting expectations is key throughout life and especially in challenging circumstances like moving. This is one of the main takeaways I hope you get from this book. Knowing what to expect so you're not completely surprised, helps immensely. It's like having a map or overhead view of a maze versus walking through the maze at ground level trying to find your way but unable to discern what lies ahead. Getting through the maze either way is work, but the first method makes it much easier to navigate. When you're more familiar with what lies ahead, you're more confident and prepared for the experience.

These things take time

Don't get frustrated if things don't feel like home immediately.
Friendships take time to develop, they don't happen overnight, so
be patient and keep encouraging your children. Transition time
varies, but setting expectations of about 6-12 months is
reasonable. Give yourself grace that first year and remind yourself
and your children to have patience as things develop (and to feel
encouraged by progress made along the way). Be realistic with
your expectations and help your children do so as well so you
don't set yourselves up for needless frustration.

Take things day by day and week by week. Set short-term goals.
When things are rough, I've always found it hard to shoot for a
long-term, distant goal (e.g., in one year from now I'll feel a lot
better, more settled in, and will have good friends). During the
first few weeks at my new schools, my goal was to make it until
the weekend. Shooting for more manageable goals can get you
through stressful times.

Some children may seem fine for the first few months and then
hit a wall where suddenly they're frustrated again. This is totally
normal. The first few weeks or months can feel very exciting, but
after some time has passed and things are okay but still not 100%
comfortable, frustration sets in. Take the time to remind your
children of how much further along they are than when you first
moved. While it may take more time and may not be immediate,
things will keep getting better.

There will be bumps in the road and it will be tiring

Understand that things will not go perfectly smooth; expect
bumps in the road. Your children may become frustrated if things
have been going well and then they encounter a setback or
challenge. They may not make the soccer team or may struggle
with one of their new classes. They may feel like they're becoming

good friends with a group of children at school and then find out they weren't invited to a party or an event that weekend. It's important to explain to them that with any great adventure there are challenges, obstacles, and setbacks. They may get a bit tired along the way, and that's okay. They have their family to help them persevere.

Picture the last time you were driving down the highway. Some sections of the road were smooth and other sections contained rough spots with potholes, cracks, bumps, debris, or even a detour. You may have seen them coming or they may have startled you. You may have tried to avoid those spots, but you can't always escape them. As with driving, during your settling in process there will be bumps in the road and just as you can't control the conditions of the road, you can't always control each stage of your transition. From time to time you may even get a flat tire and have to take a break to change that tire. But, ultimately, you don't let any of it stop you from where you're going. It's not about the bumps, it's about where you're headed: you and your family are on course for a great new life!

Make sure you take care of yourself during the settling in period. Being constantly "on" is tiring. Learning new names, faces, streets, destinations, and developing new routines, all while trying to make friends, can be exhausting. In order to fully support your children you need to take care of yourself as well. Make sure you are making friends and building your own support network.

You may feel alone, but you're not

As mentioned earlier, moving can make you feel completely alone. In fact, when I think back on my moving experiences, I vividly remember those first days at my new school. I felt like I had been pulled out of my world and then spit back into a different world while everyone else's life had been continuing on. My life had abruptly stopped and then started over again someplace else. I felt removed from my past and completely disconnected from my future.

Remind your children they left a house and school where they knew their surroundings (people, places, things) and felt comfortable with what to expect from their daily routines. They are now in a new situation where everything will be unknown at first, from how to find the bathroom to where and what to expect of school lunch hour. Assure them that feeling out of place is completely normal in the beginning as they're familiarizing themselves with the new area.

This is the point at which your children can pull out mementos and memories of their old friends to remind themselves they're cared for and not alone. Journaling and re-visiting the suggested books and movies of others struggling with a move can help as well. As C.S. Lewis once said, "We read to know we are not alone."

Lastly, remind them even though it feels like everything is new, there's also a lot that has stayed the same: their family, their belongings, who they are, and that they're loved.

The pain of the move is temporary

The overwhelming feeling which accompanies a move will pass. Each week will get better as places, people, and things become a bit more familiar. You and your children will learn where things are (the grocery store location, where the school bathrooms are, where their locker is) as you begin to settle in and you'll become more and more comfortable. My mother recalls how excited she was after our first move when someone recognized her while she was running errands and waved to her from their car. As she tells the story, "I finally felt that I knew someone then and felt more at home."

The good news is a lot of the basic logistical unknowns will be the first to dissipate. After the first few weeks at school, your children will feel more comfortable navigating around, just as they will in your new home and neighborhood. The social component will take a bit longer. Try to view each stage as its own hurdle. Early on, enjoy feeling more comfortable with logistics and celebrate the small social triumphs (someone remembering your name, striking up a conversation with you, waving to you in the hallway, or inviting you over). It's easy to overlook the progress you're making when you're living through a difficult situation. Taking time away to remember the first day, when you knew nothing and no one, enables you to see how far you've come. Encourage your children to pat themselves on the back for each step they take toward settling in.

It's going to be hard the first few months and you might feel like you'll never be comfortable or "at home." Then suddenly someone will stop you in the grocery store and say, "Does your son need a ride to practice?" or, "Is your daughter going on the field trip?" and you'll realize your family is really starting to settle in. Someone once told my family, "You'll know when you belong when you switch from saying 'going back to our house' to 'going back home'." Josh, a friend of mine, says that for him it is when someone asks him for directions in his new city and he is able to help them that he feels he has finally made the transition. There are plenty of small signs you can look for as encouragement that you're making progress. As you notice the small things, remember you're on your way to making this new location your home.

The sooner you make it feel like home, the sooner you'll be comfortable

Most of Part IV is about getting settled in quickly and helping create an environment where you and your children can best transition. There's virtually no way to get around the initial discomfort, but embracing it and quickly taking steps to get settled helps speed up the process of getting comfortable.

Try to quickly return to as many old routines as possible to balance out the newness. For example, if you always listened to the news in the morning in your last city, do so in the new city. If the children played basketball and liked it, get them on a basketball team again or set up a basketball hoop outside so they can play and interact with neighbors while doing so. If the old routines don't apply, start to build new routines. Children thrive upon consistency and feel safest when they have structure. The quicker you start to immerse yourself in the new area and community, the faster the transition will be and the sooner you and your family will start to feel a sense of belonging.

What if you're not planning on staying long in this new town? I would highly recommend treating it like you've moved there to stay indefinitely, even if this isn't the case. It's very challenging to make the effort to settle in if you keep thinking about leaving. And if you don't make the effort to settle in, it won't happen and your time there will most likely be unhappy. It can be off-putting when meeting new people if they fear you'll move away after they take the time to build a friendship with you. Remind yourselves that while you're there you need to put your efforts into making it your home. When others ask if you'll be staying, as best as you can, express your interest in remaining in the area and that you are looking forward to becoming part of the community.

Even though we moved around every two to four years, we hoped that each move would be our last. We acted accordingly and put forth the effort to get established. I spent my energy on settling in and enjoying my time there, becoming part of my community, and forming great friendships, even though I knew I'd be sad later when I would have to leave my friends. Make wherever you are your home for the sake of your family's health and happiness. It's worth the extra effort up front and the sadness at the end to have an amazing time in the middle. And ultimately, you'll be far happier than if you hold back so that you don't have to deal with the pain of future goodbyes.

No matter how certain you are, you can't predict the future, even if the job or role you accepted is short-term. You don't know if your job assignment will be extended or if another job will come up in the same area. Because you're not a fortune teller, focus on the present and settle in. We all know plenty of people in our lives who say, "You know, I was just going to live here/work here for a year and now it's five years later and here I am." What if they kept "not investing" in the area each year because they kept thinking they were going to leave soon? That would've been a long and sad five years!

Teens will face a variety of pressures and challenges in addition to those associated with moving

As previously discussed, teens are at a point in their lives where fitting in often takes top priority. It's important to realize that even without the stress of a move, teenagers can be under a good deal of social pressure from their peers. While you can't be there for them at school to "fix" things, you need to support them, and you can best do this by understanding the world in which they live.

Teenagers tend to be a bit emotional already and their reaction to the move may be unpredictable. It's easy to feel guilty, but your efforts and energy should be focused around helping them. Those first months are best spent letting them react and adjust, loving and supporting them, and keeping an eye out for any larger issues.

Understand that your teen may at some point be in a situation where he or she may be pressured with smoking, drinking, drugs, or other risky behavior. While some of this is inevitable and part of growing up, know that your teen's desire to fit in is heightened in this new situation. It will be important to be there for them.

Stay engaged with them and their lives, talk openly about how they're doing, and set clear rules for what is acceptable and allowed (you need to know their plans and who they're with for safety reasons).

- **These things take time.**
- **There will be bumps in the road and it will be tiring.**
- **You may feel alone, but you're not.**
- **The pain of the move is temporary.**
- **The sooner you make it feel like home, the sooner you'll be comfortable.**
- **Teens will face a variety of pressures and challenges in addition to those associated with moving.**

Chapter 14: Keeping in Touch

"Be well, do good work, and keep in touch." — *Garrison Keillor*

Help your children keep in touch with their old friends. Leaving friends behind was likely one of the hardest parts of the move for them. This is a great opportunity to teach them that just because someone isn't in their immediate vicinity doesn't mean the friendship has to end. Relationships change as life circumstances change, but your children will learn that with a little time and effort, those who are important to them can remain in their lives.

There are so many ways to keep in touch

With email, text, IM, and the prevalence of social media, it's very easy to keep in touch. Additionally, setting aside time for a phone call or video chat provides a great opportunity to hear a friend's voice or see their face to stay connected. If your children have a lot of friends they want to keep in touch with, remind them they can send a group email or post updates on Facebook. But, to truly stay connected with the friends who matter most, one-on-one communication is key. Despite the popularity of online communication, a handwritten letter can be a meaningful way to keep in touch from time to time. Have your children exchange addresses with their friends if they haven't done so already. They can send a letter or the occasional "care package" to share items with one another (food, small gifts, and trinkets). If your children are wondering what to say to their friends, suggest they show them the new home by sending photos or a video tour. You can also have your children describe their new school, friends, hobbies, and the places they've been. Encourage them to continue to talk about everyday things like TV shows or movies they've seen or their soccer game last week, just as they would if they were still living close to each other.

Your children should also feel free to share how they're feeling and adjusting with their friends. Remind them to be sensitive to their friends' feelings. It's hard to be the friend left behind, having an important part of your life move away, with no exciting new town or experiences to take its place. Your children should let their friends know they miss them, give them updates on how they're settling in, and ask them questions about their lives. On the other hand, it may be hard for your children to hear about their old town and friends; it may make them sad they're not there. Keep reminding them of the fun things going on in their life and the progress they've made so far.

You can even encourage your children to do something special with those they miss. They can make plans to read the same book or watch the same TV show or the same movie and then talk about it afterwards. I have a friend whose daughter made plans to read a popular teen series with her best friend after she moved away. They would then call, text, and IM throughout each book to discuss what they had read. It gave them a fun way to stay connected. Many video games let you log on and play remotely with other people as well. These shared activities create easy conversation pieces and are a way for children, who aren't inclined to sit and talk for extended periods of time, to remain close to their friends. With all of these options it's easy, with a little effort, for children to remain connected to those they left behind.

Keeping in touch with those important to you helps provide support and remind you of who you are

One of the most isolating parts of a move is showing up in a new city where it feels like no one knows you or cares for you. Staying in touch with people who do care about you can provide support while you're getting established in your new place and building a new support network. The encouragement that comes from these established relationships can help your children (and you) during your adjustment.

After almost every move, within six months my family had friends from our old location come for a visit. It was great to see them, and it was exciting for us to show them our new home and the places around town we had discovered. We felt like we had lived there forever because, for that visit, we were experts on the area.

Letting go: for everything there is a season

Bear in mind that you'll stay close with some people while others (although great people and once an important part of your life) will fade into the past. This is okay! Help your children understand some people are brought into our lives for a season. We may reconnect with them at a future point, or we may not, but that doesn't take away from the memories or the meaning of their friendship. For anyone you want to remain in touch with, you'll put in the effort to do so.

Remember, the future holds great friendships for you. There are amazing people everywhere. From central Kentucky to New York, from Chicago to San Diego, I've never moved anywhere where I didn't find great friends and a strong support network. Some places and circumstances take more time than others and the ways you meet friends may differ from place to place, but there are good people everywhere: people you'll connect with, have things in common with, laugh with, play with, and share with. You'll meet people and grow so close that it will feel like they were always a part of your life.

Take care to not let it hinder you from moving forward

While it's important to stay in touch with old friends, make sure your children aren't focused solely on that while not investing in new friendships. New friends and connections to your current location are a critical aspect to feeling settled, adjusting to the move, and accepting the new place as home. Help your children find a balance between staying in touch with old friends and making new ones. They need to be actively working to build friendships in your new location, and staying in touch shouldn't become a crutch that allows them to delay acceptance of their new home.

Making future plans to return for a visit can be beneficial

If feasible, let the children plan and look forward to a trip back to see old friends. Don't return too soon however, as you need to give your children time to focus on your new home and invest in building relationships there. Even during freshman orientation in college, many school advisers counsel parents not to let students return home until they have a chance to get comfortable with their new surroundings.

My family typically waited to visit our old home until about a year had passed to really make sure we had settled into the new home. Sometimes it can be painful to see your old home and friends when you're not yet comfortable in your new area. It can remind you of how uncomfortable you are and prolong the settling in process because it draws your mind back instead of helping you focus it forward. It can make some of the new transition pain feel more challenging than it would be without the reminder of "how it used to be". That being said, knowing they're going back for a visit, once they're feeling settled at their new place, gives your children something to look forward to. It makes the move seem less drastic when they know they'll see their friends again.

Going back to visit after some time has passed can actually help the children get additional closure. When they go back, they'll see life in their old community without them there and begin to realize that it doesn't feel like their home anymore. The image that has remained frozen in time, as it was when they left, is suddenly pitted against the reality of how it has moved on without them. This is their opportunity to start to see that the world they miss doesn't really exist in that same form anymore. It has moved on, just as they have.

- **There are so many ways to keep in touch.**

- **Keeping in touch with those important to you helps provide support and remind you of who you are.**

- **Letting go: for everything there is a season.**

- **Take care to not let it hinder you from moving forward.**

- **Making future plans to return for a visit can be beneficial.**

Chapter 15: New School

"Continuous effort—not strength or intelligence—is the key to unlocking our potential." — *Sir Winston Churchill*

Changing schools presents a real challenge for children, both academically and socially. School is where children spend the majority of their day, and it helps shape their identity. Having that aspect of their lives change dramatically is often very unsettling.

Visit to get the lay of the land

As previously touched upon, now that you are in your new home, be sure to check out your children's school with them ahead of time so their first day of school isn't the first time they are seeing it. Even if it means starting them one or two days later, it's often more beneficial to give them the opportunity to see and experience the new school before their first day so they know what to expect. If you can get your child's schedule and walk the route together ahead of time, it can help to ease some of their anxiety.

Take a tour of the school so your children can see the cafeteria, library, classrooms, gym, nurse's office, front office, where the buses drop off and pick up, the playground, etc. Let them see where everything is located so they can then focus on other things happening during their first day. Take this opportunity to learn more about any activities in which they are interested. You may be able to look at the meeting room or meet the coach. You can also inquire about any deadlines for joining a club or tryouts for a sports team (which may begin before the start of the school year). This is also a great time to find out about how lunchtime is handled: what are the options to purchase food, what time is lunch, and is seating assigned by classroom or unassigned?

Introduce yourselves to the principal if he or she is available. Ask how the school handles newly enrolled children: Do they have a club? Do they provide the children with a buddy to show them around in the first weeks? Is there a special first day orientation they'll attend? If they don't have a buddy system in place, request one and see if they can provide a peer as a friendly face to show your child around.

Additionally, if you can, meet with any of your children's teachers or coaches (either during that visit, another time before starting, or shortly after starting). Introduce yourself to the teachers and let them know your child's strengths and weaknesses, as well as what he or she was working on in the old school district. This will help to determine if the move has caused any curriculum gaps. Depending upon your children, you can let their teachers know the areas they may need help with upfront or let the teachers assess them on their own. Either way, plan to meet with their teachers a few weeks into the transfer. My mother always made an appointment with my sister's Language Arts/English teacher about three or four weeks into the move to see how she was progressing. My sister often struggled with Language Arts and my mother wanted to let the teacher know, but first she wanted the teacher to evaluate my sister without bias.

Communicating with the teachers will enable them to help your children transition. It will also give them a head's up to look out for your children during those first few months when they most need the attention. Finally, this will create a relationship between you and the teachers. Your children's teachers will be with them throughout the day and may observe any adjustment issues that arise which you might not notice at home. If you stay in periodic contact with their teachers, you'll get a better feel for your children's adjustment and the teacher will also feel more confident in giving you feedback.

Prepare for the first day

As other parts of the move come to a close, it will be important to re-visit and make sure you are prepared for the children's first day at school. Inquire about what information you'll need to enroll your children in their new school (transcripts, physical, immunization records) and what supplies they'll need. Also ask about the dress code and any other school-specific information you might need.

Your children may have concerns about how they'll be getting to school. It's important to them that they know what time school starts, bus routes and times, along with parking or unloading if you're dropping them off. Ask your children if they want you to drop them off at school on their first day and walk them in or if they would prefer to take the bus. Let them state their preferences for the first day, and when the time draws near, go over the specifics of the plan with them. If they're catching the bus, show them where the bus stop is and tell them what time the bus will come. Walk or drive by the bus stop so they can see it, and practice the route with them so they will feel confident about how to get there. This can include pointing out landmarks along the way so they can re-trace their steps.

Lunchtime is often unstructured and very social and thus may be a cause for concern for some children. Looking back, who I would sit with at lunch was usually my biggest worry before my first day of school. With the research you've done so far, you can help your children plan ahead for what to expect. Suggest that during the class before lunch they look around and find a friendly face and ask him or her either during class or on the way to lunch if they can sit with them. If your children are too nervous to ask, suggest they strike up a conversation with the other children and walk all the way to lunch and then naturally sit together.

Over and over again, I hear lunch come up as significant concern with new students. One young girl recently told me that she and her mom created three plans for her first day so that she felt more confident going in. Plan A, her best case scenario plan, was to find a friendly face during class and ask to sit with them at lunch. Plan B was that if she hadn't found anyone to sit with her during class, she'd look around the cafeteria after arriving and find someone sitting alone who looked friendly and she could approach. Plan C, her worst case scenario, concerned what to do if she couldn't find someone and couldn't handle sitting alone. She would then ask for a pass to go to the library.

Every student is unique, and this student needed plans laid out so that she felt less nervous going in to the situation. Your child may or may not want that type of structure but the story shows the stress that the first few lunch hours can cause children. This young girl actually told a teacher about her strategy while reflecting back on her first day a few months in to the school year. Her teacher liked the idea so much that she now councils all new students who ask her advice with the Plan A/B/C lunchtime strategy.

There will be a lot of new information for your children to remember. Help them by coming up with tricks to memorize or locate important information. Mnemonics for their address, bus, teacher's name, etc. will help them prepare (e.g., "I am 8 years old and I take bus #8"). If they get lost while at school, remind them to reach out to others (students, teachers, other adults at school) for directions or any other questions they may have.

Prepare for differences in curriculum

We talked a bit about the best time to enroll your children in school and how to note any gaps and catch up on missing parts of the curriculum, in Chapter 4. It's important to keep this in mind and to be on the lookout for any differences during and after enrollment. When you enroll your children, provide the new school with all pertinent information from their former school to help ease the academic transition. As previously stated, teachers and administrators at most schools believe their school district is better than your previous district. They will likely want to run their own assessments and tests on your child. A child who places into the gifted curriculum at one school might have to be tested again at the new school to qualify. While this is frustrating, it's likely to happen. My family never encountered a school district that fully trusted the previous district's assessments. You should still bring all your children's test scores, especially standardized ones as those supersede any local and district specific biases and will clearly convey your child's overall abilities.

If you're dealing with teens in high school, keep in mind how the move will impact their transcripts when they apply to college. Moving around is a fact of life and shouldn't hurt your child's ability to get into the college of his or her choice. However, it's important you take steps to make sure credits and classes transfer to the new school accurately and that any conversions are done fairly. One high school may offer different honors or AP classes than the other or may have different requirements for classes like gym, art, or health. Work with the new school to find the best transition for your child. Each situation will be unique, but you can't blindly trust everything will be converted fairly.

Schools, like organizations, often believe their way is the best and only way, or that converting things is too much effort. Don't rely on the new school putting any effort into comparing the old school's classes to their own. Do it for them by giving them all the information they need (requirements, curriculum, classes taken, grades and grading scale used). Almost every school I attended had a different grading scale. For some schools a 93% was an A, for another it was a B+ and A's started at 94% and above. Some had a 4.0 grading scale but honors and AP classes were based on a 4.5 or 5.0 scale. My first high school substituted a varsity sport for gym class but my next high school required gym and wanted me to catch up on my "missing" credits when I enrolled. Fortunately, this was accomplished by taking gym class during summer school so it didn't interfere with academic courses during the regular school year.

I have a friend, Lisa, who reflects back to her high school move where she went from a school on the quarter calendar system to one using trimesters. She had worked hard to be on track for early graduation at her first school, but lost quite a few credits during the transfer, had to re-take several classes, and was unable to graduate early. Although it may seem like a small thing, she still remembers feeling disappointment and frustration that all she had worked for was lost because of the move and her family not taking the opportunity to work with the school to compromise.

If your child previously took honors biology and there is no honors biology in the new school, the new school may try to adjust the grade to fit their standard class. It's important you work with the school to transfer your children's transcripts and GPAs so they accurately reflect their work in high school and not let their past efforts be lost in the shuffle of the transition. The conversion won't be perfect and you'll need to compromise in some areas. Be creative and flexible and do your homework ahead of time so you go into this process informed on both schools' policies, and don't be afraid to respectfully stand your ground.

Finally, be sure to provide both schools' information with your teenager's college applications so the college understands the differences between the schools' requirements, grading scales, and academic structures. A conversation with an admissions counselor at a university in San Diego highlighted the importance of doing this. Her advice holds true for all schools: if you don't make your transcripts easy for the college to understand (for any type of move, but especially for international moves), there's a good chance your child's application may be overlooked. The college may not have anyone with the time to investigate how the different schools translate, so help them out with that information.

Stay connected, especially in those first months

Keep the lines of communication open with your child and with the school so that you can touch base regularly and gauge how your child is adjusting. Continue to ask your children how things are going. Do they like their classes and classmates? How are they finding the new school and teachers? As far as your involvement in the school, ask your children (especially if they're in middle or high school) what they would be comfortable with. Respect their requests but remain active in their lives so you know how they're doing. If they don't want you to volunteer for field trips or other activities in which you'll be interacting with them and their friends at school, they may accept that you'll still attend their sporting events or volunteer elsewhere (the library, the concession stand or school store, etc.) to remain connected.

Even if you don't have time to volunteer, the most important part is maintaining a relationship with their teacher(s) so you can check to make sure everything is okay. Teachers are around your children and able to observe not only their school performance but also how they appear to be adjusting and interacting with their classmates. They've seen numerous newly relocated children and can likely give you a knowledgeable assessment of how your child is adjusting compared to other transferees.

A high school history teacher once relayed a story of a family who had just moved from Connecticut to Kentucky and was in one of her classes. The boy's mom emailed her a few weeks in, noting that her son was new and struggling with the transition. This teacher's class also coincided with lunch hour and thus was an especially important time socially and the teacher immediately recognized this. Now that she had been made aware of the boy's struggles she found another friendly, outgoing boy and changed her seating chart so she could move them next to one another. The two boys became good friends and ended up sitting together at lunch as well. "Most teachers feel a lot of sympathy for new kids. That's why we are teachers, because we like kids!" she explained to me. "Parents just need to let us know and they'll be surprised at what we can arrange. We can find potential friends and either sit them near one another or put them together for group work."

As the first few weeks pass, work with your children and their teachers to make sure they were placed in the correct class levels. On several occasions I was placed in lower levels and told I had to work my way up. Calling attention to and letting the teachers know your goal can help expedite this process. Conversely, your child may have been placed in a level too high and is having trouble keeping up. I can remember a similar situation in my eighth grade Spanish class. If you believe this is the case you have two options: If the level is higher than your child is ready to handle, especially given the stress of the move, investigate the class level below to see if it would better meet your child's needs. If you and your child believe the level is appropriate but that he or she has missed a piece of the curriculum the new school has already taught, your child will need to work to catch up. The teacher may be able to provide the information needed for your child to catch up, or you can hire a tutor or work with your child yourself to help them. In Spanish class I befriended the girl who sat in front of me and she helped me to identify what I was missing. Then I set about making flash cards and putting them up throughout the house so I could see them as I walked around.

Whichever path you choose, it's important to make sure your child is in the appropriate class for his or her level. This may not happen immediately, but keep diligently monitoring your children's progress and remember that you can work things out over the next few months. It may not all be perfect the first week. Trust your children to help you understand how much they can handle as well.

- **Visit to get the lay of the land.**
- **Prepare for the first day.**
- **Prepare for differences in curriculum.**
- **Stay connected, especially in those first months.**

Chapter 16: Making Friends

"Friendship is born at that moment when one person says to another: "What! You too? I thought I was the only one." — C.S. Lewis

"I've learned that people will forget what you said, people will forget what you did, but people will never forget how you made them feel." — Maya Angelou

When people hear I moved a lot growing up, they usually ask questions that have to do with making friends. Was it hard to make friends? How did you make friends? Making friends is a common concern and is an area that will often cause the most anxiety and require the most effort, but it will also finally make you feel as if you belong. As your children grow older, friends become increasingly important in their lives, so be aware your children may be concerned about making new friends after the move. Will they be accepted? Will they be able to connect with people the way they did with their other friends?

Encourage your children to think about what they want in a friend

Our friends and the people we surround ourselves with have a significant impact on how we think, how we act, and what we believe. While many friendships naturally develop around us, we do have control over who we associate with. Teaching your children how to assess their values and what's important to them will help them see how they can take control and responsibility for who they let into their lives. You can talk this through with them or encourage them to journal about it. Your children should understand this isn't a search for perfection but rather an opportunity, while being respectful of others, to choose who to become close with.

Encourage your children to think about what makes a good friend, what they like to do, and what they're looking for in a friend. This can serve as a foundation for meeting and befriending new people. I value independence, self-confidence, humor, intelligence, and not being swayed by the crowd, so growing up and throughout my adult life I've looked for others who share similar values. My sister values athleticism and physical activity, humor, imagination, respectfulness, and loyalty, so she would always select friends who fell in line with those criteria, knowing they would have things in common which mattered the most to her.

Remind your children the friends they want in their lives are those with whom they genuinely connect and who will support them and make them feel good about themselves overall. Their goal is to find people with whom they can laugh and share their feelings and experiences. They shouldn't try to fit in with a group, they should find friends with whom they naturally fit. During my first few days of school I would usually be friendly and approachable, yet take the time to watch how the other students interacted with one another. I looked for the person who treated others well and who seemed to be the type of person I wanted in my life.

In each school there is the popular clique, the "in" crowd, the cool kids, the A list. Your child, like others, may want to be acknowledged by or be a part of the popular groups. This is fine if that group is a good fit and a healthy influence on them, but too many children try to fit in with this group and find being rejected by them can hurt.

As you talk to them about how to select friends, continue to emphasize being themselves and finding people who accept and like them for who they are. Even if they're accepted by a popular group, they may find things aren't as exciting as they appeared from the outside. During one move in junior high, I found myself in a group that was often cruel to outsiders. When I began to see this and figure out they weren't the type of people I wanted to associate with or could trust, I learned a bit about myself and what mattered to me.

Remind your children of the importance of being true to themselves and to their values. No friend worth having will ask them to compromise on this or pressure them into situations which are unhealthy or would get them in trouble. Instill the importance of taking the time upfront to surround themselves with the right people, and live this out in your own life as an example for them to follow.

Suggest your children take the initiative to introduce themselves

I once got a fortune cookie that read, "A wise man makes his own luck." Your children (and you!) need to take chances and create opportunities to make friends. Let them know that they can sit back and wait for people to approach them (and some will) or they can move things along and quickly establish themselves by reaching out to others. While it may feel more comfortable to let others approach, they're then left waiting for others to act. They know they need friends, so encourage them to take the initiative and say hello.

As you meet people in your neighborhood, introduce yourself and let them know you have children and what ages they are. If you set an example for your children on how to take the initiative and meet people, they may be nervous to do so, but once they've seen you make the first contact a few times and get the feel for it, they will feel a bit braver. If there are children of a similar age in the neighborhood, encourage your children to meet them so they'll have friends to be with when they're not at school. This is especially helpful for younger children.

Remind your children to introduce themselves at school as well. They can strike up conversations with those seated near them in class (before or after class, of course!). When I would find classmates who seemed nice, I would sit near them or ask them questions about homework to establish a relationship and see if we connected as friends. If your children are still uncomfortable initiating conversations, remind them to, at a minimum, be sure to make eye contact and smile so they seem approachable and open to meeting others.

Quick tips. The poet Ovid once said, "If you want to be loved, be loveable." I think the version of that quote for this chapter could be, "If you want friends, be friendly." If your child is nervous or needs some tips to help make friends, you can go over the following steps with them (and use them yourself):

1. **Act confident**: Even if your children don't feel confident, they can act the part. Confidence isn't arrogance, defensiveness, or acting as if you're better than others. It's being secure with yourself and comfortable with who you are. When we feel nervous in a given situation, acting confident will often make us start to feel more confident.

2. **Ask questions and be a good listener**: Tell your children to balance talking about themselves with asking questions about the person they're talking to and to take a genuine interest in what they have to say. Remember, most people love to talk about themselves. Allowing them to do so will make the conversation easier and allow your children to learn whether the person shares their values.

3. **Make eye contact and smile**: Be approachable. Even if your children don't feel like smiling, forcing a smile will often make them feel happier and as a result, make them seem friendly, which will increase the odds of others approaching them.

4. **Be aware of other's reactions and responses**: While your children need to take initiative in meeting others, remind them not to be pushy and to be aware of when others aren't interested in talking and respect their privacy.

5. **Be trustworthy and loyal**: Tell your children to be the type of friend they would want to have and not to criticize, gossip, or judge others.

And finally, a bonus tip always worth repeating: **Be yourself!**

Appearing friendly and positive will attract friends. While it is normal for your children to make negative comparisons between their old and new school, it may be worth having a conversation with them to tell them to keep those thoughts in their head or to express them to you and your family, but not to share regularly with other students.

A high school teacher once conveyed to me that she cringes when she sees new students fall into the negativity trap of comparing everything to their old school, making it clear that nothing is as good as their former home. She watches as it turns off the other students, who then think that the new student believes they are too good for others. Teaching your children to present themselves in an open and approachable manner will help them make friends and start to feel at home sooner.

Meet people with common interests

An easy way for your children to meet and connect with friends is to join a group or activity they enjoy. Getting involved will also provide your children with a sense of belonging in the community, so they'll feel included and a part of the group. Ask your children what clubs they would like to join. It could be anything: sports, hobbies, clubs (music, crafts, theater, Girl/Boy Scouts), or even summer camp. Getting your children involved with extracurricular activities allows them to meet another set of peers, in addition to those at school, with whom they have the opportunity to connect based on shared interests.

You can also coach a team or volunteer as a leader to get your children into an activity they like. This also helps with meeting new people. More often than not, my parents would volunteer to coach or lead teams and groups we wanted to join as a way to get us involved with the group. This is not my parents' natural inclination and I doubt it would have happened if we hadn't moved, but they saw it as a good way to get us involved. During one move, my mother was told the Girl Scout troop was full but then they mentioned they needed a leader. My mother volunteered to lead, and I was able to join the group. She used to say that sometimes you need to be creative in finding ways to make a place start to feel like home.

Be open

Remind your children to stay true to who they are but not closed off to new experiences and new ways of doing things. As stated previously, moving is a great time to evaluate what's important to you in a friendship and the types of friends you're looking for. Be open and try not to pre-judge.

In the beginning they're simply looking to connect with people and to get to know them. Then, as time goes on, they'll find those with whom they connect the most. You and your children shouldn't put pressure on yourselves to feel that you have to find great friends right away.

First impressions aren't always correct. I can think back to great friends I've had throughout my life who, if someone had told me when we first met that we would become close, I would never have believed it (and vice versa). Remind your children to stay open-minded as they get to know people. Sometimes the people you least expect will surprise you and end up becoming your closest friends. If you close yourself off to those opportunities and write people off early on as not "your type," you'll miss out on some really great friendships.

Encourage your children to be open and friendly with everyone they meet, realizing that it's okay if some people they interact with early on don't become their close friends. It's seldom a waste of time to get to know people, especially when you're new.

Don't be discouraged, it takes time

Your children may feel lonely in the beginning and tired from always having to be "on" and approachable as they start to make new friends. It takes courage to make new friends, so continue to encourage them. If they want to take control, help them create a plan to make friends and get involved in activities. Have them write the plan down and put it where they can see. They should set specific short-term goals (join a club, attend a meeting, smile at five new people) that advance the long-term plan.

Take the time to talk with them about the progress they're making and celebrate how far they've come. It will take a few weeks for your children to start making friends, and then some months for those friends to go from casual friendships to closer friendships like the kind they (and you) had in your old town. Remind them they won't be the new students forever and each day brings them closer to becoming more established.

Use your "adventure plan" to organize activities for them during the first few weekends if they haven't made friends yet or feel disconnected from school. Additionally, remind your children they shouldn't be shy about speaking with their school guidance counselor or another adult at school if they're having a hard time making friends. Guidance counselors are often an under-utilized resource and may be able to provide a different perspective on how to get to know children at school.

Children also need to be told to not take things too personally. It's easy when you don't have friends and are taking steps to reach out to others to become discouraged and overly hurt when you feel rejected by someone who isn't as open to a new friendship. Continually let them know not to be afraid to take chances. With each experience they can learn, make adjustments, and get back at it. I'd rather be the type of person who has the confidence to try reaching out to others, realizing I won't be successful every time, than the person who worries about being perfect and therefore avoids trying anything new.

Not every person will become a good friend, but your children won't know until they try. It's healthy to reach out to others even if it doesn't result in a friendship. As your children get to know someone, it may turn out that that person isn't as good a friend as your children thought he or she would be. They can adjust to this and although it may feel like starting from scratch as they move on, it's not. They've already made a lot of progress in getting familiar with their surroundings and shouldn't be discouraged that the social aspect will take a bit longer.

I often hear different regions of the country labeled as "friendlier" than others. While we did find in a few of our moves that this would sometimes be true, there are actually warm and welcoming people everywhere. Sometimes they'll approach you, sometimes you'll need to approach them, but my many moves taught me they're out there. From the East Coast to the Midwest, from the South to the West Coast, there were always friendly faces ready to make us feel welcome.

Sometimes we would move to schools that were used to transplants, where every year a large group of new students would start together. Conversely, while living in the suburbs outside of New York City, I attended a junior high school where everyone had grown up together from a young age. New students were an anomaly; a phenomenon not many knew what to do with. I can remember feeling so frustrated and hurt the first few days. Why were none of the other students speaking to me or inviting me to sit with them?

This wasn't like my previous experiences at other schools. I had to make a concerted effort to talk with them, ask them questions, and walk out of class with them so I could casually start a conversation. I had never worked as hard to make friends before in my life! Fast forward one year to my birthday party. I had a wonderful, close group of friends and lots of great acquaintances. A few friends from that time told me how they remembered my first day of school, thinking that I looked nice and wanting to meet me but just weren't sure how. I couldn't believe it. I was the new girl who didn't know anyone and they were the ones who were nervous! It was an eye opening experience which still serves to remind me that just because someone is not introducing themselves to me doesn't necessarily mean they're not friendly or open to meeting new people.

Most children are friendly and welcoming. However, although unlikely, bullying can happen anytime and anywhere, and new children may be susceptible as they don't yet have their full support network in place. Let your children know it's never acceptable to bully others and that if they're being bullied it isn't their fault. Keep the lines of communication open so they feel comfortable sharing with you or another adult.

- Encourage your children to think about what they want in a friend.

- Suggest your children take the initiative to introduce themselves.

- Meet people with common interests.

- Be open.

- Don't be discouraged, it takes time.

Chapter 17: The Trailing Spouse

"What lies behind us and what lies before us are tiny matters compared to what lies within us." — *Oliver Wendell Holmes*

While much of the advice given in this book applies to both children and adults, it is important to recognize that the trailing spouse (the spouse whose job did not necessitate the move) may face unique difficulties once the move has occurred. He or she is often making the move without a built in group (like school for the children) or a job in which to transition. While working to get the family settled in their new home, the trailing spouse may also feel isolated and find it challenging to quickly create a sense of belonging for his or herself.

If you're the trailing spouse, recognize you'll encounter some additional challenges as you support your family throughout this move. Much of the advice contained in this book may be helpful in dealing with your own transition (even as you're helping your family through theirs). Don't neglect your own feelings as you go through the process. You'll need community support and encouragement just as much as your children, and it's critical you find support for yourself so you can give your children all the love and assurance they require during this period.

As an adult, get involved to make friends

The fears and worries children have about making new friends are not dramatically different from those we feel as adults. And the effort in making new friends and taking initiative is also similar in many ways. Therefore, you have a good opportunity to help your children learn how to make friends by sharing your own feelings, experiences, and advice. It may be more difficult for you to make friends at first as you may not have a place, such as school, to meet people, and you'll be busy setting up your new home.

The spouse whose job initiated the move may be working longer hours as he or she gets oriented with the new job, leaving the other spouse with more responsibilities at home and more alone time. Remember, parents often have the opportunity to make friends by meeting the parents of their younger children's friends. This becomes more difficult as your children get older and more independent. But regardless of how old your children are, there are always opportunities for you to meet people. As you get your children involved in extracurricular activities, sit at their practices and talk to the other parents. This is also a great time to solicit advice on the area. For those working outside of the home, the office can be a natural place to meet friends as well.

Some of the easiest and quickest friendships to make are with other recently transplanted people. They, like you, are trying to establish new friendships. Check if there are any "Newcomer Clubs" in the area. It's easy to connect with other people who've also moved and often provides a great support network. You can bond over common frustrations and pleasant surprises you each encountered during the move.

Be careful not to spend too much time with those who are particularly unhappy and not applying themselves to making this new location their home. My mother remembers a move where she spent time with another woman whose family had just moved to the same city. The woman's constant complaining and unhappiness reinforced all the negative things my mother didn't like. After a while, my mother came to realize this woman was keeping her from moving forward in the new location. A support network needs to support the right behaviors.

Getting involved is the key. Don't just sit at home! Join groups, volunteer, attend "Newcomer Clubs," or start one yourself. Don't wait for people to invite you to things, be willing to go to events and places on your own and meet people there. Volunteer at your children's school or chaperone their field trips (with the added benefit that you'll also get to know the area!). Join groups or attend activities which align with your interests in order to meet people with whom you have things in common. It really can be as simple as, "Hi, my name is Jane/John, what's your name? I just moved here and thought I'd try out this group." Follow up with a question. You can ask them if they're from the area, inquire about the group meeting times or upcoming activities, etc. Meetup.com is a great resource to find people with common interests if you're new in town.

Even consider signing up for lessons when you might not need them, as classes and clubs are a great way to get to know more people. My aunt moved to a new city and was shopping in a cooking supply store when she saw that they were having cooking classes that following week. She was a very good cook, but signed up anyway as a way to meet people in the area with common interests and ended up meeting one of her closest friends.

Consider taking on a leadership role (treasurer, coordinator) within the group. You can't help but get to know people and feel a sense of belonging when you're organizing or involved with the operations of the meeting. And remember the wise words of Dale Carnegie, "You can make more friends in two months by becoming interested in other people than you can in two years by trying to get other people interested in you."

Understand your social environment

As our personalities take shape and we grow older, our lives begin
to revolve more and more around social components. How others
react to the "new person" can have a strong impact on our lives.
As you and your children meet new people, you'll interact with
different personality types. There seem to be five main types of
people I've encountered as a teenager and as an adult, each of
whom have a different pattern of interaction:

Wanda/William Welcoming: This person is immediately excited
to meet you, often taking it upon him or herself to come up to
you and make an introduction. They usually empathize with your
situation (either from having been there and remembering what it
felt like, or just naturally recognizing the difficulty you face). They
will go out of their way to be friendly, look out for you,
proactively provide helpful information, invite you to things, and
introduce you to people. It will come as no surprise the Wanda
and William Welcomings of the world make the transition much
smoother and more comfortable. I can still remember people
from all of my moves who fall into this category, and I'm still
deeply grateful to them and for the role they played in my life at a
time when I needed their help the most.

Susie/Sam Slightly-shy: This personality type is harder to get to
know in the beginning. These people probably won't approach
you and when you approach them they'll be hard to read at first.
You may not be able to tell whether or not they're interested in
being friends because they may seem distant, quiet, or standoffish.
If you keep being friendly, but not pushy, Susie or Sam Slightly-
shy will often open up and become a great friend. They're either
unsure of how to introduce themselves or they hold off until
they've had time to evaluate who you are. Don't be disheartened
by the fact that they're not approaching you and providing as
much help as a Welcoming personality. Susie and Sam Slightly-shy
are great people and would love to help you settle in if you're
patient and give them the chance.

Nancy/Nate Needy: This is a smaller group but they can end up taking up a lot of your time if you do encounter them, as they often gravitate to new people. They may thrive on drama, wallow in negativity, always need the spotlight, or be determined to help and then control you and others. They go through friends fairly quickly and thus newcomers are a source of new friends for them. If given the opportunity, Nancy and Nate Needy will drain your time, energy, and emotional well-being.

While we all have insecurities, theirs guide their behavior but are well hidden at first. They're great for a while because they bring friendship to your new life. She's the friend who wants to relate to you by complaining. He's the friend who needs to be the center of attention at all times. She's the friend who swoops in to help and welcome you but as time goes by seems to want to control you. He may be the friend whose poor decisions and unhealthy relationships regularly take front and center stage and eclipse all else.

If you find yourself giving and giving and feeling more and more drained, you may be friends with a Nancy or Nate Needy. You probably won't notice at first, but it will become evident over time. Friends support each other, but you'll come to realize this relationship is mostly about them getting their needs met. Respectfully pull away from the unhealthy relationship so you can take care of yourself.

Elizabeth/Edward Established: Those in this group have their own lives established and, for whatever reason, at this time are not particularly open to or interested in making new friends. They may be very welcoming at first but then suddenly stop their efforts or they may not even take that first step. Don't take offense to their seeming disinterest in you. You have no idea what's going on in their lives. They may be busy dealing with family, personal, or career matters. They may have a packed schedule with no time or interest in stepping away, or a select few may truly be uninterested in making new friends at this point in their life. In fact, I've heard people in my own life at different times, including extended family members, say they have enough friends and aren't interested in making any more. When I would hear people say things like this I used to get angry at the callousness of dismissing others who might be in need and considered them to be self-absorbed.

Elizabeth and Edward Established used to really frustrate me. But I've learned that in most cases Elizabeth and Edward are good people. If their life is too hectic to introduce new people into it, then there's nothing you can do about it. Be friendly and when things calm down in their life they may end up becoming your friend. If they happen to be truly disinterested in meeting new people, you can't do much about that either and they're not the type of people you want in your life anyway. Given the choice, I like to hang out with people who are empathetic to those around them, welcoming, and inclusive!

Tina/Trevor Threatened: This is a small group but, as I've seen them pop up consistently in every move I've made and routinely hear about them from friends and family in new situations, they're definitely worth discussing. This person, as you probably have guessed from the name, views you as a threat. Or, probably more appropriately worded, feels threatened by the disruption of the status quo. People like to know where they stand and where they fit in.

Some people define themselves by their status, so when you, as a new person, enter into the picture, it temporarily disrupts the order of things while people figure out how and where you'll fit into the broader picture. Will you be smarter than them, better at sports, more popular with friends or the opposite sex, better at theater or music, or funnier than them? Will you run for the position they want in a group or organization? Threaten their role at work? Your newness and your yet unknown position in the order of things is a threat, and they may react rudely, dismissively, or in a downright cruel fashion in response to their unease.

Again, this is a small group of people, but unfortunately, meeting a person like this is often a reality in a new situation. It helps to know why these behaviors are occurring and that it's not actually personal (even when it feels very personal). While you don't want to move into a new situation so aggressively you turn people off, you also should never compromise who you are. Go in seeking to learn and be respectful, but be yourself. Try hard, shine in your areas of expertise, go for what you want, and recognize that ultimately what these people are reacting to is the uncertainty of where you'll fit into their world. Once you find your spot, they'll frequently adjust to it and will calm down and accept you. Their reaction will often occur whether you're a real threat to them or not, as is usually the case. They're reacting to the unknown and not to the facts. Give them time for things to become known. You can't win them all over, so in the midst of any run-ins you may have with a Tina or Trevor Threatened, focus on finding yourself a good group of friends who accept and support you and vice versa.

As you make friends, remember, your new friends have other established friendships. It's important you don't become jealous of them or expect to be included in everything they do, but rather make yourself open to meeting them and expanding your circle of friends. On the flip side, some of those people might become jealous of your new friendship with their friend, especially if they don't know you or don't know you well. Meet them, reach out to them, and hang out with them too. Remember, friends of friends are more likely to be a good fit for you also (if you like your friend, odds are you'll like their friends as well!). This isn't to say you have to like them or want to embrace all of your newfound friends' other friendships, but it's often a good way to meet people.

~~~~~~~~~~~~~~~~~~

Keep a positive attitude

Now that you've made the move, keep repeating to yourself that a positive attitude is still a decision and a daily choice. Each day you can choose to face the situation anew and view it as an adventure and an exciting opportunity. Your children will take notice and it will help them to adjust. To convincingly encourage your children to think positively, you'll need to do it yourself. If you're finding that to be a challenge, it may be important to take a step back and assess how you're doing with the move and what could help and encourage you. Make sure you have a personal support system in place so you can be a support to your children. Lean on the support of friends and family as well, even if they aren't geographically close they will want to help you get through this time.

Both you and your spouse need to be fully committed to the move! It will be too stressful on your relationship and on the children's transition if you're not on the same page. You need to support one another, as well as your children, during this process. No matter who was more in favor of the move, once the decision has been made, support one another during each step and openly communicate your needs and expectations. Define the roles you'll each play in helping your family get through the transition (e.g., which of you will research the new location, which of you is better at handling feelings and fears and can help the children process theirs).

Settling into a new area can be really exciting, but it can also be really rough and cause you to lose sight of things in the midst of the stress, chaos, and sadness. It's so easy to slip into negative thinking during a move, especially as time has gone on and the newness and excitement starts to wear off. Dale Carnegie once wrote: "It isn't what you have, or who you are, or where you are, or what you are doing that makes you happy or unhappy. It is what you think about." Thoughts like, "I will never feel at home here," "I will never find the kind of great friends that I had in the last place," or "The last place was so much better because. . ." can become self-fulfilling. At the very least, they can drag out the length of your adjustment time. Take control of your mindset when you find this happening and work to:

✔ *Smile and laugh.* Remember to smile and laugh. It's a great cure for stress, sadness, boredom, and loneliness. Watch a funny movie or TV show. Appreciate the humor in life. Still struggling? Even a forced smile has been shown in some studies to help decrease stress!

✔ *Focus on the good and appreciate what you have.* Continually remind yourself of what's most important and try to re-focus daily on your family, loved ones, and health. Focus on the small accomplishments, the progress you're making, and what you appreciate in life. I've heard different variations of this daily "count your blessings" advice. Every night, especially during the tough times, my father would tell us to say three things we were thankful for or that went well that day. It could be as simple as the weather, having food to eat, or someone inviting you to sit with them at lunch. You can encourage your children to do this at dinner, at night before bed, or to write it in their journal, and do it yourself when things get tough. Although very simple, there's power in appreciating what we have. It helps shift our focus away from negativity.

✔ *Think of things as an adventure.* You've been given the chance to explore a new area, try new things, and meet new people. As discussed in earlier chapters, focus on the opportunities the move brings.

✔ *Set up reminders and encouragements.* During the times in my life (moving or not) when I've been very stressed and struggled to maintain a positive mindset, I've posted notes around my room or house to remind myself of how I wanted to think. In high school, when I moved to a new school with a much better tennis team, I was very nervous I wouldn't make the team. My parents and sister were traveling during the week of tryouts, so I was at home alone and progressively getting more and more panicked about my skills and abilities. Because I was new, I wasn't able to talk things out with anyone else on the team, so my thoughts and fears began to spiral. I remember thinking, "I want to make or not make this team based on how skilled I am. I don't want my fears to get to me and affect my performance and have them be the determining factor."

I decided which things I needed to do to remain in control during tryouts and wrote them on sticky notes where I would see them each day. I put one on my bathroom mirror and one on the door frame of my room. I can't remember the exact list, but SMILE was #1, "Take deep breaths" was #2, and #3 went into the technical components I wanted to work on for my tennis serve. I needed gentle reminders to regain control of my mindset and not let the fear win.

If anxiety and fear become overwhelming, create an action plan and follow it so you're not paralyzed with terror. You'll take control, move closer to your goal, and feel accomplished as you complete the small steps in your action plan.

✔ ***Do something nice for someone else.*** Finally, it's good to remember that sometimes when we're sad we become too self-focused and need to pull ourselves out of it. Doing something nice for someone else helps take the focus off of you and your struggles and will usually cheer you up as well. It can be as simple as just smiling at a stranger on the street to brighten his or her day. Or you can even "pay it forward" and look for others who have also moved to the area to help them settle in. Additionally, volunteer work often provides opportunities to appreciate how well off we really are and enables us to meet new people. We are wired for community and consequently we feel rewarded when we help others even in the midst of our own struggles.

- As an adult, get involved to make friends.
- Understand your social environment.
- Keep a positive attitude.

Chapter 18: Creating a Sense of Belonging Wherever You Are

"When you're curious, you find lots of interesting things to do." — Walt Disney

"Twenty years from now you will be more disappointed by the things that you didn't do than by the ones you did do. So throw off the bowlines. Sail away from the safe harbor. Catch the trade winds in your sails. Explore. Dream. Discover." — H. Jackson Brown Jr.

There's nothing like moving somewhere and feeling like you don't fit in. It makes you feel uncomfortable and many times it manifests in the way you act and carry yourself, separating you from others. The best way to address this is to make a concerted effort to create your own comfort zone and sense of belonging in your new city. Go out and explore, get involved, be flexible, and take the initiative to form a group if you cannot find one you like!

Be a tourist

Enjoy the opportunity to be a tourist in your own city or region. No matter where you've moved, there will be new and interesting things to see. This is good advice at any age. Research and make a list of all the fun things nearby your new home that you want to do or see. Reference tourism books, travel websites like TripAdvisor, and your city's tourism website or office for ideas to add to your to-do/to-see list. You can put anything on the list, from landmarks and restaurants, to festivals and events, to neighborhoods and stores. It's entirely up to you and your family. Asking for other's opinions is an easy way to start a conversation as well. You can introduce yourselves and ask for recommendations of things to do around town ("We've just moved in and have been trying to get to know the area. Anything you'd recommend we see or do? Any good restaurants you'd recommend?"). You can also ask for their opinions of things already on your to-do list. This also gives you the opportunity to share your experiences. Most people will love to hear what you've done and enjoyed so far in their city! And recommendations create a natural follow up conversation topic as well: "Thanks for your suggestion on that great Italian restaurant for dinner. We went there last night and loved it."

In checking things off of the list, you become more familiar and thus more comfortable with the area and will also have things to do on the weekend if you haven't yet made friends or joined any clubs. Let it be a "filler" so you and the children aren't sitting at home bored and wishing you were back in your old house where you had friends and things to do. It also lets you try things specific to or popular in your new area and experience things you wouldn't have otherwise.

When I lived in the suburbs near New York City, I saw my first Broadway show and visited the Statue of Liberty. In Kentucky, I learned about horse racing and the Derby and enjoyed the beauty of the rolling hills and horse parks. In upstate New York, my newfound friends taught me to ski and all the families in my neighborhood got season passes to nearby slopes. We would spend our weekends skiing with friends and sitting in the lodge drinking hot chocolate and eating massive chocolate chip cookies (a personal favorite of my friends and mine at the time).

In Philadelphia, I learned to play lacrosse. My family also visited any surrounding historic sites that were within a day trip, more times than I can count (which I appreciate more now than I did growing up). In Chicago, I joined a tennis team and the coach really inspired my passion for the sport. In Cincinnati, we lived close to the city and would frequently go downtown for shows, plays, and sporting events. No matter where you are, there will be interesting things to do and try.

Make the most of your free time

One of the complaints we all have, no matter who we are and where we live, is how hectic and busy our lives can become. We're strapped for time and often find ourselves with a full schedule. Moving temporarily frees up our calendars. Although we're busy with the move and logistics of settling in, other areas which used to take up our time are now missing (activities, organizations, friends). We may find ourselves with the first free weekend we've had in a long time. While this void may feel empty, remind yourself it won't be long until your calendar is full, so embrace it while you can. How often have you wished for a day or weekend with nothing you "had to do?" How did you want to use that time? Take this "free time" to work toward your goals while it is available. Take advantage of this time to really reflect on how you want to build your new life. Be selective in what you do and what activities you choose to join.

Encourage your children to do this as well. It could be exploring your new area, taking classes, picking up a new hobby, volunteering, or spending more quality time together as a family. In some of these activities you'll run into others who have similar interests and this also will help you make friends, settle in, and establish yourself.

Keep an open mind and seek to learn

Whether you're moving to another country or moving to another part of the United States (that at times may seem like another country), make the decision to give it an honest try. Almost every place will have its quirks and do some things differently than other places. Though, at times, you may feel like it is something out of *The Twilight Zone*, your goal should be to respect these differences. This doesn't mean compromising who you are or giving up your preferences. This just means accepting that the new place does things a bit differently. If something isn't illegal, morally offensive, or against your values, is it really worth putting the energy into fighting an entire system just because it's not what you're used to?

As you settle in, you'll likely start to notice more and more of these differences. Some may even be improvements, but there will also be differences that you don't like ("I liked how the old school's calendar was set up better than this" or "I liked our old shopping center much more than this one"). While these feelings are often inevitable, it's important to remind yourself to avoid negative comparisons. There are some differences that you'll need to accept and there will be others for which you'll need to find alternatives. Either way, recognize that some of your frustration is stemming from the "newness" of everything in your life and that you may be channeling your overall frustrations into annoyance at a few particular items or places.

Think back to a time when you were somewhere you belonged and a new person came in who was uncomfortable or unfamiliar with the group or area. If that person was standoffish or rude, constantly explaining how things didn't make sense or weren't being done right, what impression did you get of that person? Did the negativity make you more or less likely to want to engage with him or her? You'll have more energy to enjoy life and appear more open and approachable to others if you're open to your new experience. You can joke with your old friends about the differences and challenges in adapting, but try to keep a positive attitude and be open around your new friends.

When finding groups and organizations to join (a daycare group, an exercise class, church/temple/synagogue), don't be too picky at first. Decide what's most important to you, start with that, and be open-minded to other things. You probably won't find something that is 100% perfect and identical to your old life. The important thing is getting back to a normal life as quickly as possible. Over time, you'll either find a better fit or grow more comfortable with the choice you made.

Follow the local news, root for the local sports teams, and take part in local festivals. These are also ways to connect with the area and with others. Some things you'll actually end up liking; others you may not but at least you'll know for sure. New experiences round out all of our personalities and help us know ourselves better (and often make for good stories after the fact!).

If you are tempted to think that just being in a location means you are experiencing it, think again. Take a moment to imagine two glasses of water. In one glass you drop an Alka-Seltzer® tablet, still in its original wrapper. In the other glass you drop an unwrapped Alka-Seltzer®. Put those glasses side by side and they will look quite different, with the unwrapped tablet's glass showing signs of life and activity. Though both tablets are "in" the water, only one is really immersed in it and interacting with it. Try to engage with your new surroundings and let down some of your "protective wrappings" to take in your new home and truly giving things a chance.

Create comfort

If you miss an aspect of your old area (a club or group that doesn't exist in your new city), consider taking the reins and starting one yourself or start a "Newcomers" group and connect with and help support other families like yours. It's really easy! Meet a fellow transplant and agree to go to a sports event or dinner. Ask if he or she knows anyone else who's new to the area who might like to be invited to a "Newcomers" activity. It can be simple and informal, with no strings attached.

In one of my family's moves there were several pre-school aged children at our church so the mothers started a "Mommy and Me" group and would meet every other week to let their children play together while the moms got some well-deserved grown-up time. This was an unstructured social time to get to know each other and provide friends for their children. They rotated homes so they learned the area and had an opportunity to welcome the other moms into their new homes, entertaining on a miniature scale and connecting at the same time.

There's no need to sit around missing things when a little bit of work and some initiative would bring them back. This also helps set an example for your children that you can step up and create what you're missing in a new situation.

- **Be a tourist.**
- **Make the most of your free time.**
- **Keep an open mind and seek to learn.**
- **Create comfort.**

CONCLUSION

There are situations that occur in our lives that will take time to get through. They may require some extra effort in adjusting to them. We all face these times. They're inevitable and often help shape our character and lead us to our most important relationships. Moving is one of these times. This book provides many suggestions for how to smooth your transition. I truly hope some are relevant to your situation and help you and your family with your move.

Being flexible, open to new things, patient, and honestly communicating will take you a long way in your transition. For families with children, it's especially important to be observant of how your children are adjusting. Include them, listen to them, and give them support.

Getting back up and moving forward is extremely important in relocations and in life. Learn from your mistakes throughout the process without punishing yourself, as these are lessons that will help you throughout your life. Most of what I learned about moving, I learned through trial, error, and experience.

Most importantly, remember the feeling of being new and be sure to welcome and help others in the same situation after you become established. My sister said she always remembered the feeling of being the new girl. In college she made a point to introduce herself and talk to new students just joining groups she was part of because she remembered what it felt like to not know anyone. Always keep in mind how grateful you were to those who reached out to you or how much you wished someone would've helped you and then be that person to someone who needs your help!

APPENDIX I

Research Studies on the Effects of Moving

The US Census Bureau stated that 37.1 million Americans aged one year or older changed residences in 2009.[2] While we may know how many people move each year, research on the impact of those moves has been sparse and inconclusive at times and notably hasn't uncovered traumatic results, other than in isolated instances (which are frequently coupled with additional family stress such as financial trouble or divorce).

A 2010 article in the *New York Times* entitled, "Does Moving a Child Create Adult Baggage?" brought to light a question that causes anxiety for all parents who've moved or considered moving their families. The article talks about the potentially negative social and academic impacts that moving might have on children, and concludes that ultimately the answer is not a simple yes or no. Delving into the complicated nature of moving, the article asserts that where efforts are made to ease the transition for children, the negative effects of a move are often neutralized.

Two researchers in particular have evaluated the research conducted over the past decades. A 2006 study by Christine McLeod concluded that the research to date on the impact moving has on children is ambiguous. She states that, "Findings on the effects of geographic mobility have been mixed with positive, negative, and neutral outcomes found in both military and civilian populations."[3] A second study by psychologist

---

[2] "U.S. Census Bureau Reports Residents Move at Higher Rate in 2009 After Record Low in 2008," United States Census Bureau Press Release, May 10, 2012.

[3] "Changing Places – Resilience in Children Who Move," Christine McLeod, University of Sydney, SID: 0213911, March 2006.

Frederic Medway in 2002 found that, "Although relocation to a new community can cause children to be anxious, to develop behavior problems, and to have academic problems in the classroom, those problems are typically short-lived. Most normal children ultimately handle moving transitions well. Those who do not handle moving well typically have problems that are present before the move rather than as a result of the relocation." He goes on to conclude that, "Successful child relocation depends heavily on the behavior and attitudes of the adults in the home and on children's opportunities to make new friends within a supportive environment."[4]

---

[4] "Best Practices in Assisting Relocating Families," Frederic J. Medway, University of South Carolina, 2002.

APPENDIX II

Settling In Checklist

✓ Check furniture, major appliances, and all boxes to make sure everything arrived (and is undamaged)

✓ Set up utilities, cable, internet, and phone services

✓ Update your mailing address with the post office

✓ Contact your insurance companies (household, auto, health), bank, investments to update your address

✓ Register your children in school

✓ Get your driver's license, license plates, register your vehicle if you have moved to a new state

✓ Register to vote

✓ If your bank does not have convenient branches in your new location, consider switching banks

✓ Sign up for local newspapers, a library card, any other local resources

✓ Find a doctor, dentist, vet and any other needed medical professionals as well as identify the nearest hospital and urgent care center

✓ Begin to ask others or research places of worship, hair salons, mechanics, and any other needs that you will regularly use

Acknowledgements

I would like to thank my family for their stories and endless support, without which this book would never have come about:

Tom Boehm, Sharon Boehm, Ashley Boehm, Diane Rollinger

Thank you again for being patient and helping me organize my thoughts.

In addition I want to thank these great friends for their thoughts, insights, and edits:

Wes Sapp, Kerri Sapp, Andrée Sosler, Noelle Seybert, Christie Asselin

I would also like to thank my editors Mandi A. Vartenuk, who helped refine and perfect this book, and Sarah Chesnutt, who did an incredible job with the final clean up and edits to ensure this book was ready for release.

Made in the USA
Lexington, KY
09 May 2018